By the same author

Selection Examination English Tests
Junior English Guide
Haydn Richards English Workbooks
Haydn Richards Junior English
Verbal Reasoning Tests Explained
More Verbal Reasoning Tests

© *Haydn Richards 1960*
Fifty-first impression 1998

Junior English Revised (without answers)
ISBN 0 602 20557 3

Junior English Revised (with answers)
ISBN 0 602 20558 1

Published by Ginn and Company
Prebendal House, Parson's Fee, Aylesbury, Bucks HP20 2OY
Ginn on the Internet http://www.ginn.co.uk

Printed in Great Britain at the University Press, Cambridge

PREFACE

This book has a dual aim—to teach and to test English.

It contains lists of the parts of speech, opposites, synonyms, homonyms, proverbs, abbreviations, idioms, etc. which every pupil should memorise before leaving the Junior School, for these are the tools which are essential for the speaking and writing of correct English.

As it is partly a reference book, the various topics dealt with have been so labelled that they can readily be found, and in order to make reference still easier the list of contents has been arranged alphabetically.

The tests have been devised to provide ample practice material of the various kinds met with in modern examination papers.

The twenty Comprehension Tests, carefully graded according to difficulty, help to develop the ability to understand what is read, an accomplishment of the utmost importance in the present age.

H.R.

CONTENTS

Thousands of years ago, when people wished to send a message to somebody, they drew pictures to show what they meant; this was because they had no alphabet, so they could not write words and sentences. Perhaps you have seen some of the picture-writing used by Native Americans?

The pictures were easy to draw and to read, as you will see from the examples given below.

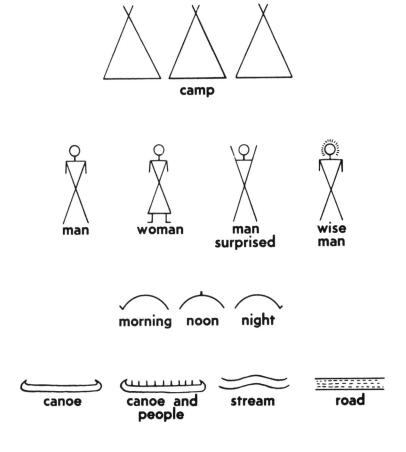

camp

man   woman   man
surprised   wise
man

morning   noon   night

canoe   canoe and   stream   road
people

But think how long you would take to send a message if you had to draw everything instead of writing words. It is much easier to **write**: "The dog chased the cat up a tree" than to **draw** a dog chasing a cat up a tree.

9

Nouns

> A word which is used to represent some object, such as man, canoe, tree, camp, dog, etc., is called a NOUN.

If you look around you, you will see many common things which have simple names:

Examples: **door; pen; desk; book; ink.**

EXERCISE 1

Write the names of six things you can see in the following places:

1. Your classroom
2. A railway station
3. A grocery shop
4. A large shop
5. A school workshop
6. A zoo
7. A fair
8. A busy seaside resort
9. A street in a busy town
10. A school canteen

Remember that **nouns** are the names of things.

EXERCISE 2

Read these sentences through carefully, then make a list of all the **nouns** you can see in them.

1. The boy lost his football.
2. The woman gave the dog a bone.
3. Did the cat scratch your hand?
4. Yesterday I ate an orange, an apple and a banana.
5. The monkey ate all the nuts which the children gave him.
6. The fireman climbed the ladder and saved the child.
7. The teacher showed the class a boomerang.
8. We watched the kitten playing with a ball of wool.
9. The eagle has a hooked beak and curved talons.
10. The robin is a brown bird with a red breast.

EXERCISE 3

Write the names of:

1. Three wild animals
2. Three farmyard animals
3. Three vegetables all beginning with the same letter
4. Three summer sports
5. Three tools used by a carpenter
6. Three occupations
7. Three wild flowers
8. Three coins used in Britain
9. Three toys for young children
10. Three kinds of meat

EXERCISE 4

Here are the meanings of ten **nouns,** all of which begin with the letter **S.** Write these ten **nouns.**

1. A seat for a rider on horseback
2. A male deer
3. The three-leafed plant which resembles clover and which is the national emblem of Ireland
4. The eggs laid by frogs or toads
5. A kind of shoe consisting of a sole secured to the foot by straps
6. A group of fish
7. A person who carves or models statues
8. A kind of bucket for holding coal
9. The bony framework of the human body
10. Another word for "pigs"

Plurals

A noun which refers to a **single** person or thing is SINGULAR in number.

Examples: boy; book; loaf; woman; tooth

A noun which refers to **more than one** person or thing is PLURAL in number.

Examples: boys; books; loaves; women; teeth

> **SINGULAR** means **ONE**
>
> **PLURAL** means **MORE THAN ONE**

You will notice from the examples given that PLURALS are formed in various ways.

1. By adding **s** to the SINGULAR

Examples: girls   tables   windows   flowers

2. Nouns ending with **s, sh, ch** or **x** form their PLURALS by adding **-es.**

Examples: boxes   foxes   bushes   brushes
glasses   asses   arches   stitches

3. Nouns ending with **y,** before which there is no vowel, form their plurals by changing the **y** to **i** before adding **-es.**

Examples: berries   cities   collieries   colonies
companies   diaries   factories   injuries

EXERCISE 5

Write the PLURAL nouns shown by the pictures below.

EXERCISE 6

Insert in each sentence the PLURAL form of a noun which ends with -y.

1. There were lovely red —— on the holly trees.
2. We saw wild —— galloping on the open moor.
3. —— lay their eggs on the underside of cabbage leaves and these hatch out into caterpillars.
4. The committee consisted of four —— and five gentlemen.
5. The cyclist received serious —— when his cycle collided with a car.
6. Many people write in their —— of what they do each day.
7. Thousands of —— are used to carry goods by road.
8. *Treasure Island* is one of the most thrilling —— ever written.
9. London, Birmingham and Leeds are large —— in England.
10. Robin's favourite —— are woodwork and stamp-collecting.

4. Nouns ending with -y, before which there is a vowel, form their PLURALS by adding -s only, as in Rule 1.

Examples:	key	day	toy	guy
	keys	days	toys	guys
	boys	monkeys	donkeys	chimneys
	turkeys	jockeys	kidneys	pulleys
	journeys	holidays	trolleys	buoys

5. Some nouns which end with -f form their PLURALS by changing the -f to -v and adding -es.

Examples:	leaf	loaf	shelf	wolf
	leaves	loaves	shelves	wolves
	thief	sheaf	calf	half
	thieves	sheaves	calves	halves

Remember that a few nouns ending with -f do not follow this rule but merely add -s.

Examples: chiefs   gulfs   waifs   hoofs   handkerchiefs

Plurals

If the noun ends with -fe the -fe is changed to v and -es is added.

Examples: wife   life   knife

wives lives knives

EXERCISE 7

Complete each sentence below by using the PLURAL form of a noun ending with f. In every case the f is changed to v before adding -es.

1. The baker made over a thousand —— of bread.
2. Butchers use very sharp —— to cut up meat.
3. The hunters heard the howling of a pack of —— in the distance
4. In autumn many trees shed their ——.
5. Last night —— broke into the stores and took a large quantity of goods.
6. The children watched the farmer carting his —— of corn.
7. At Christmas time the —— in the sweet shops are laden with chocolates and sweets.
8. A man who has two —— at the same time is called a bigamist.
9. Maisie, the cow, gave birth to two ——.
10. Two —— are equal to a whole one.

6. Nouns ending with o form their PLURALS in two ways, some by adding -s, others by adding -es.

By adding -es	By adding -s
torpedoes	pianos
potatoes	solos
heroes	banjos
cargoes	Eskimos
tomatoes	sopranos
volcanoes	curios
echoes	dynamos

7. Several nouns have no SINGULAR form. We never speak of a **scissor,** or a **trouser,** but always of **scissors** or **trousers.**

Examples: braces   barracks bellows breeches

shears   pants   tongs   pincers

shorts   gallows pliers spectacles

14

8. Certain nouns have the same form for SINGULAR and PLURAL.

Examples: one sheep   one deer   one salmon
           many sheep   many deer   many salmon

9. The PLURAL number of some nouns is formed by changing a vowel or by adding **-en.**

Examples: foot   man   goose   ox   child
          feet   men   geese   oxen   children

10. The PLURALS of some compound words are formed by adding **-s** to the first word.

Examples: son-in-law   passer-by   maid-of-honour
          sons-in-law passers-by maids-of-honour

EXERCISE 8

1. Write six nouns which form their plurals by adding **-s,** e.g. door–doors.

2. Give six plurals formed by adding **-es,** e.g. thrush–thrushes.

3. Write six plurals formed by changing **y** to **i** and adding **-es,** e.g. baby–babies.

4. Write six nouns ending with **f** in which this letter is changed to **v** when **-es** is added.

5. Give three nouns ending with **f** which merely add **-s** to form their plurals.

6. Write three nouns which have the same form for both SINGULAR and PLURAL.

7. Give three nouns which have no SINGULAR form.

8. Write three words ending with **o** which form their PLURAL by adding **-s,** and three nouns ending with **o** which add **-es.**

Plurals

EXERCISE 9

Rewrite the following sentences, changing the **singular** nouns in heavy type into the **plural** form, and making other necessary changes.

Example: The **lily** is a beautiful **flower.**

Answer: **Lilies** are beautiful **flowers.**

1. The **boy** made an **entry** in his **diary.**
2. The hunted **fox** hid in the **bush.**
3. The **baker** put the burnt **loaf** on the **shelf·**
4. The rich widow left her money to her **son-in-law.**
5. Sergeant Smith arrested the **thief** this morning.
6. The **thief** ran off down the alley.
7. The soprano sang a **solo** at the concert.
8. A heavy mist hung over the **valley.**
9. The **builder** promised to mend the **roof** tomorrow.
10. The **buffalo** was chased by a **lion.**
11. The **peasant** gathered in the **sheaf** of corn.
12. The **urchin** raced along the **alley.**
13. The audience listened to the **lady** playing the **piano.**
14. We failed to find the **atlas** in the library.
15. The **policeman** could not solve the **mystery.**
16. The **torpedo** sank the **ship.**
17. The farmer will kill the **goose** and the **turkey** for Christmas.
18. The **child** knocked over the **vase.**
19. The cheese had been gnawed by the **mouse.**
20. The **woman** played with the **baby.**

EXERCISE 10

Insert the correct **plural** in each space below.

1. one knife — three ——
2. one chimney — several ——
3. one pulley — many ——
4. one half — two ——
5. one crutch — a pair of ——
6. one pansy — a bunch of ——
7. one sheep — a flock of ——
8. one foot — two ——
9. one wolf — a family of ——
10. one donkey — five ——

16

Collective Nouns

a **herd** of deer

a **flock** of sheep

Noun	Collective Noun
actors	company
aeroplanes	flight; squadron
angels	host
arrows	sheaf; quiver
bananas	bunch; hand
bees	swarm; hive
bells	peal
birds	flock
bishops	bench
books	library
bread	batch
buffaloes	herd
cards	pack
cattle	herd
chicks	brood
china	set
cigarettes	packet
clothes	suit
corn	sheaf
cotton	bale; reel
dancers	troupe
diamonds	cluster
directors	board
drawers	chest
eggs	clutch; sitting
elephants	herd
fish	shoal
flowers	bunch; bouquet
friends	party
furniture	suite
grapes	bunch
grass	tuft
hay	stack; truss
horses	team
insects	swarm; plague
islands	group
kittens	litter

Noun	Collective Noun
labourers	gang
lions	troop; pride
locusts	plague
magistrates	bench
minstrels	troupe
monkeys	troop
musicians	band
oxen	team
pearls	rope; string
pictures	collection
pilgrims	band
pupils	class; school
pups	litter
rabbits	nest
rags	bundle
sailors	crew
savages	horde
servants	staff
ships	fleet; flotilla; squadron
silk	skein
singers	choir
spectators	crowd
stamps	collection
stars	cluster
steps	flight
sticks	bundle
stones	pile; heap
swallows	flight
teachers	staff
thieves	gang
tools	set; kit
trees	clump; forest
whales	school
wolves	pack
worshippers	congregation

Collective Nouns

Write the correct **collective noun** in the spaces below.
1. There is a new —— of furniture in the lounge.
2. A steep —— of steps led to the artist's studio.
3. At sunset a large —— of trawlers put out to sea.
4. Nigel received a fine —— of tools for his birthday.
5. Jennifer presented the Queen with a —— of flowers.
6. Mr. Jackson smokes a large —— of cigarettes every day.
7. There is one playing-card missing from this ——.
8. The author has a large —— of books of all kinds.
9. The baker burnt the first —— of loaves.
10. Peter pitched his tent under the —— of trees.

Insert a suitable **collective noun** in each of the spaces.

1. a —— of grapes
2. a —— of matches
3. a —— of clothes
4. a —— of trees
5. a —— of corn
6. a —— of drawers
7. a —— of beads
8. a —— of sticks
9. a —— of stamps
10. a —— of stars
11. a —— of birds
12. a —— of cows
13. a —— of angels
14. a —— of wolves
15. a —— of mackerel
16. a —— of whales
17. a —— of bees
18. a —— of monkeys
19. a —— of thieves
20. a —— of pups

Write the **collective noun** indicated by each of these pictures.

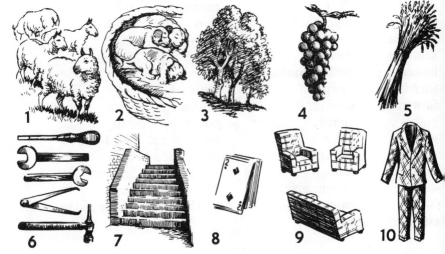

EXERCISE 14

March, June, April and **May** are all **months.** Give the group name for each line of words below.

1.	potatoes	turnips	carrots	beans
2.	chisel	hammer	pincers	pliers
3.	cruiser	schooner	liner	destroyer
4.	autumn	spring	winter	summer
5.	pork	mutton	beef	veal
6.	water	petrol	milk	vinegar
7.	violin	harp	trumpet	piano
8.	Asia	Africa	Europe	America
9.	measles	mumps	diphtheria	leprosy
10.	penny	shilling	sixpence	florin

EXERCISE 15

To each line below add another word which belongs to the same group. Write also the name of the group.

Example: **spear   rifle   sword   (revolver, weapons)**

1.	duck	goose	chicken	——	——
2.	church	cinema	museum	——	——
3.	corgi	greyhound	spaniel	——	——
4.	wheat	oats	barley	——	——
5.	butter	lard	sugar	——	——
6.	yellow	green	blue	——	——
7.	France	Russia	Italy	——	——
8.	cup	saucer	plate	——	——
9.	peach	pear	apple	——	——
10.	daffodil	rose	carnation	——	——

EXERCISE 16

One word is out of place in each group below. List the odd words:

Example: **table   bookcase   settee   window   stool**
Answer: **window**

1.	captain	corporal	major	colonel	lieutenant
2.	cobra	frog	lizard	adder	copra
3.	painter	chauffeur	typist	optimist	optician
4.	hockey	golf	chess	rugby	cricket
5.	car	bus	plough	taxi	lorry
6.	rifle	sword	spear	revolver	saw
7.	wood	oil	stone	coke	coal
8.	shilling	florin	sixpence	cheque	penny
9.	slippers	pullover	skirt	blouse	coat
10.	piano	violet	violin	viola	trombone

19

Group Names

Which word in the right group belongs to the group on the left?

1. nephew	mother	aunt	***	foreigner	cousin	adult
2. diamond	emerald	ruby	***	sapphire	brooch	pearl
3. cardigan	pullover	coat	***	curtain	cushion	skirt
4. oak	ash	birch	***	beach	helm	beech
5. fly	wasp	bee	***	worm	gnat	spider
6. shoes	slippers	boots	***	gloves	mittens	sandals
7. grocer	butcher	baker	***	draper	miser	soldier
8. lark	thrush	robin	***	goose	turkey	wren
9. herring	hake	cod	***	mackerel	lobster	cockle
10. cupboard	chair	table	***	wardrobe	carpet	stove

EXERCISE 18

From each line below select the word which is the **group name** for the other words in that line.

1. sparrow	robin	thrush	bird	starling
2. apple	fruit	plum	peach	pear
3. herring	mackerel	plaice	haddock	fish
4. tree	ash	oak	elm	sycamore
5. potato	turnip	vegetable	carrot	cabbage
6. lead	gold	iron	metal	copper
7. pork	meat	beef	mutton	veal
8. autumn	summer	season	winter	spring
9. hammer	chisel	screwdriver	tool	spanner
10. colour	orange	yellow	green	black

EXERCISE 19

Give the name of the **group** to which the following belong.

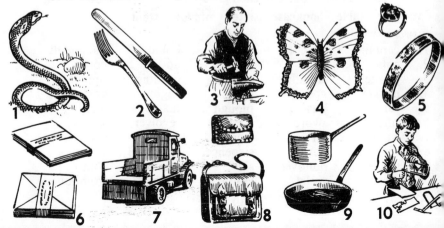

Gender

Masculine	Feminine	Masculine	Feminine
abbot	abbess	landlord	landlady
actor	actress	lion	lioness
bachelor	spinster	lord	lady
baron	baroness	male	female
beau	belle	man	woman
boar	sow	manager	manageress
boy	girl	manservant	maidservant
bridegroom	bride	marquis	marchioness
brother	sister	masseur	masseuse
buck	doe	master	mistress
bull	cow	Mr.	Mrs.
bullock	heifer	mayor	mayoress
cockerel	hen	monk	nun
colt	filly	murderer	murderess
conductor	conductress	nephew	niece
count	countess	papa	mama
dog	bitch	peacock	peahen
drake	duck	prince	princess
duke	duchess	proprietor	proprietress
earl	countess	rajah	ranee
emperor	empress	ram	ewe
executor	executrix	shepherd	shepherdess
father	mother	sir	madam
fox	vixen	sire	dam
gander	goose	son	daughter
gentleman	lady	stag	hind
giant	giantess	stallion	mare
god	goddess	steward	stewardess
governor	governess	sultan	sultana
grandfather	grandmother	tailor	tailoress
headmaster	headmistress	tiger	tigress
heir	heiress	traitor	traitress
hero	heroine	uncle	aunt
host	hostess	viscount	viscountess
hunter	huntress	waiter	waitress
husband	wife	widower	widow
king	queen	wizard	witch
lad	lass		

Gender

Look at the sentence below.

My uncle and aunt gave the poor child a fivepenny piece.

Uncle is the name of a **male** person. (*he*)

Aunt is the name of a **female** person. (*she*)

Child can be **either male** or **female**. (*it*)

Shilling is **neither male** nor **female;** it has no sex. (*it*)

Nouns which refer to **males** belong to the **masculine** gender.

Examples: man; father; king; son; emperor; postman, etc.

Nouns which refer to **females** belong to the **feminine** gender.

Examples: woman; widow; daughter; hen; girl; queen, etc.

Nouns which refer to **either males** or **females** belong to the **common** gender.

Examples: teacher; cousin; sheep; orphan; baby; pupil, etc.

Your teacher may be either a man or a woman; your cousin may be either a boy or a girl. The words do not denote the sex.

Nouns which are **neither** of the **male** sex nor of the **female** sex belong to the **neuter** gender.

Examples: book; door; stone; sky; desk; football; mountain, etc.

EXERCISE 20

Copy these words in your exercise book, then write after each the letter which shows its gender. Write **M** for masculine, **F** for feminine, **C** for common and **N** for neuter.

Examples: **aunt** (F)   **son** (M)   **sock** (N)   **child** (C)

1. niece	8. nun	15. mistress
2. husband	9. bride	16. monk
3. spade	10. film	17. secretary
4. scholar	11. lawn	18. motor-car
5. nephew	12. princess	19. friend
6. bull	13. traveller	20. host
7. guest	14. hotel	

EXERCISE 21

The nouns which denote the following persons belong to **the masculine** gender. What are they?

1. the son of a king
2. a man or boy who has done a very brave deed
3. a man who has never been married
4. a man whose wife is dead
5. a man who serves customers in a restaurant or hotel

These nouns belong to the **feminine** gender. Write them.

6. a woman who is about to be married
7. a woman who is supposed to have magic powers
8. a female who will inherit property after a person's death
9. the woman in charge of a school
10. a woman who has never married

Now write these nouns of the **common** gender.

11. a child whose parents are dead
12. a person who is received and entertained at another's house
13. one who writes books, stories, etc.
14. a person who is being treated by a doctor

The last five nouns are **neuter** in gender.

15. the floor of a fireplace
16. the iron block on which a blacksmith hammers red-hot iron
17. the instrument used to take photographs
18. the bat used in tennis
19. a stretch of land entirely surrounded by water

Gender

In the following, change each **feminine** noun to the **masculine** gender.

Example: The **widow** decided to marry again.

Answer: The **widower** decided to marry again.

1. The princess appeared at the palace window.
2. Hissing angrily, the goose made towards the children.
3. Henry's grandmother is very fond of him.
4. The cow was grazing contentedly in the meadow.
5. The bride arrived early at the church.
6. The landlady of the hotel was most obliging.
7. Sally has two tame rabbits, both does.
8. The waitress brought me a plate of steaming soup.
9. The old white duck led the procession down to the pond.
10. The mare was being harnessed for the first time.

EXERCISE 23

Now change each **masculine** noun into the **feminine** form.

1. The tiger snarled as the jackal approached her cubs.
2. The little colt was just over three months old.
3. The piglets kept close to the boar.
4. The headmaster was very pleased with the examination results.
5. The king was mourned by millions of loyal subjects.
6. The proprietor of the guest house was French.
7. Mrs. Yardley sent her nephew a handsome birthday present.
8. The old man worked very hard in the shop.
9. The rams raised their heads as we entered the meadow.
10. The heir is expected to inherit a large fortune.

EXERCISE 24

Insert the word **opposite in gender** to that in heavy type.

1. The **Duke** and —— of Camford attended the annual ball.
2. The letter began: Dear **Sir** or ——.
3. There were several —— and ewes in the field.
4. The huntsmen caught the **fox,** but the —— escaped.
5. Victor is spending a holiday with his **uncle** and —— in Scotland.
6. There were flowers for the **ladies** and cigars for the ——.
7. Mr. Carter has seven children, four **sons** and three ——.
8. So John Ridd and Lorna Doone became —— and **wife.**
9. Grazing in the park were two deer, a **stag** and a ——.
10. The St. Bernard **dog** is larger than the ——.

Compound Words

Many words are made up of two smaller words joined together.

Examples: **house** + **wife** = **housewife**
                    post + **card** = **postcard**
                    bull + **dog** = **bulldog**

A word which consists of two smaller words joined together is called a COMPOUND WORD.

EXERCISE 25

Write the ten **compound words** indicated by these pictures.

EXERCISE 26

What are the **compound words** indicated by the meanings below.

Example: **A man who lays bricks.**   *Answer:* **bricklayer.**

1. A shop in which some kind of work is done
2. A person who sells milk
3. One who makes watches
4. A tray which holds tobacco ash
5. A cloth which covers a table
6. A house in which coal is stored
7. One who keeps a shop
8. The lines at the head of a newspaper
9. A shelf on which books are kept
10. The place where roads cross

25

Compound Words

In each of the exercises below write the words in Column A in the order shown, then add on a word from Column B to form a **compound word**.

	I			II	
Column A	**Column B**		**Column A**	**Column B**	
1. home	berry		1. hand	light	
2. shoe	hole		2. water	board	
3. book	hog		3. steam	worm	
4. back	sty		4. butter	jack	
5. key	chair		5. moon	cuff	
6. blue	work		6. silk	cake	
7. hedge	bone		7. side	cup	
8. arm	bell		8. play	proof	
9. straw	lace		9. oat	ship	
10. pig	mark		10. lumber	ground	

Each missing word in these sentences is a **compound word** beginning with **foot-**. Write the complete words.

1. Soccer is played with a round foot****.
2. A foot*** is a male servant who answers the doorbell in a mansion or large house.
3. A foot**** is a path used only by pedestrians.
4. Robinson Crusoe found foot****** in the sand one day.
5. Mother puts her feet up on a foot***** when she rests.
6. Shoes, boots, sandals, slippers, etc. are called foot****.
7. A boxer's foot**** often gets him out of trouble in the ring.
8. The detectives could hear foot***** on the garden path.
9. The row of lights at the front of a stage are called foot******.
10. People crossed the river by means of a foot******.

Possessive Nouns

Long ago, when a boy wished to show that a book belonged to him he wrote something like this on the inside of the front cover.

Henry Baker, His book.

Today we would write: **Henry Baker's book.**

The apostrophe (') shows that the letters **hi** are omitted.

The apostrophe is now used for nouns of all genders.

> the **boy's** head   (*masculine*)
> the **girl's** hair   (*feminine*)
> the **child's** nose   (*common*)
> the **week's** work   (*neuter*)

Singular Nouns   To show possession, write the noun which indicates the owner, then add **'s.**

Note that the **s** is never joined to the noun.

EXERCISE 29

Write the **possessive** form of these nouns:

1. clown	6. teacher	11. cousin	16. tiger
2. father	7. parent	12. friend	17. matron
3. dog	8. conductor	13. robin	18. nurse
4. workman	9. monkey	14. doll	19. Richard
5. month	10. captain	15. tortoise	20. soldier

EXERCISE 30

Instead of saying **the fleece of the sheep** we can say **the sheep's fleece.**

Write each of these phrases in another way, using the **possessive** form of the noun.

1. the claws of the cat	6. the ears of the donkey
2. the horns of the cow	7. the beak of the pelican
3. the antics of the clown	8. the wings of a fairy
4. the antlers of the deer	9. the nest of the blackbird
5. the fangs of the cobra	10. the Ship of Her Majesty

Possessive Nouns

Plural Nouns   If the plural noun does not end with **s**, add **s** as in the case of singular nouns.

Examples: the **Women's** Institute
the **men's** football boots
the **children's** playing-fields
the **oxen's** tails

If the plural noun ends with **s,** write the apostrophe after the **s.**

Examples: the **boys'** classroom
the **lions'** manes
infants' clothing

EXERCISE 31

Write the **possessive** forms of these plural nouns:

1. parents	6. ladies	11. children	16. teachers
2. men	7. women	12. foxes	17. firemen
3. boys	8. birds	13. babies	18. dogs
4. sailors	9. eagles	14. kittens	19. workmen
5. miners	10. cooks	15. wolves	20. charwomen

EXERCISE 32

Rewrite these phrases so as to introduce the **apostrophe.**

1. a club for boys
2. the cloakroom for ladies
3. a meeting for teachers
4. a canteen for workers
5. a paddling pool for children
6. overcoats for men
7. the classroom for girls
8. helmets for firemen
9. whistles for policemen
10. the League for Women

EXERCISE 33

Write out the following sentences, inserting the **possessive** form of the noun given in brackets at the end of each.
1. The —— leg was broken in the accident. (**cyclist**)
2. The —— meeting was held in the staff room. (**teachers**)
3. The —— tail was 15 centimetres long. (**mouse**)
4. The —— face was wet with tears. (**baby**)
5. We did not see the —— signal. (**policeman**)
6. This drawing is a —— work. (**pupil**)
7. The clinic has large stocks of —— foods. (**babies**)
8. The —— concert was most amusing. (**pupils**)
9. Our —— welfare should always come first. (**country**)
10. We stayed three days on our —— farm. (**cousins**)

EXERCISE 34

Insert the **apostrophe** where required in the sentences below.
1. The boys pulled a thorn out of the dogs paw.
2. Michael sometimes wears his fathers shoes.
3. Hopeful and Christian were shut up in Giant Despairs Castle.
4. Most children have read Alices Adventures in Wonderland.
5. Two apes were pulling the monkeys tail.
6. Henrys parents paid for the firemens services.
7. The wind blew away peoples hats.
8. The rabbits tails were short and fluffy.
9. I saw that cats whiskers twitching.
10. Oliver Twist was taken to Fagins den.
11. The referees whistle was lost in the players dressing-room.
12. Mr. Morris said that the girls work was better than that of the boys.
13. Mr. Morris said that the work of both boys and girls was very satisfactory.
14. The horses had their tails plaited with ribbons.
15. The horses tails were plaited with ribbons.
16. A group of rooks nests is called a rookery.
17. The rooks nest in trees.
18. The children admired the soldiers smart uniform.
19. The farm workers disturbed a wasps nest.
20. Some of them were badly stung by the wasps.

Forming Nouns

Verb	Noun	Verb	Noun
abolish	abolition	compose	composition
accept	acceptance	confide	confidence
accompany	accompaniment	confuse	confusion
accuse	accusation	congratulate	congratulation
acquaint	acquaintance	conspire	conspiracy
act	action	construct	construction
admit	admission	converse	conversation
	admittance	correct	correction
adopt	adoption	create	creation
advertise	advertisement	deceive	deceit
advise	advice	decide	decision
allow	allowance	declare	declaration
appear	appearance	defend	defence
applaud	applause	defy	defiance
apply	application	deliver	delivery
approve	approval		deliverance
arrive	arrival	depart	departure
ascend	ascent	depend	dependence
assist	assistance	describe	description
attract	attraction	destroy	destruction
begin	beginning	discover	discovery
behave	behaviour	disturb	disturbance
believe	belief	divide	division
betray	betrayal	encourage	encouragement
bore	boredom	enter	entrance
calculate	calculation		entry
cancel	cancellation	exclaim	exclamation
choose	choice	exhaust	exhaustion
circulate	circulation	exist	existence
clean	cleanliness	expect	expectation
clear	clearance	expel	expulsion
collect	collection	explain	explanation
combine	combination	explode	explosion
commence	commencement	explore	exploration
communicate	communication	expose	exposure
compare	comparison	extend	extension
compel	compulsion	fly	flight
compensate	compensation	grieve	grief
complain	complaint	grow	growth
complete	completion	hate	hatred

Forming Nouns

Verb	Noun
hinder	hindrance
imagine	imagination
imitate	imitation
inform	information
injure	injury
inquire	inquiry
intend	intention
interfere	interference
introduce	introduction
invade	invasion
invent	invention
invite	invitation
judge	judgment
know	knowledge
laugh	laughter
lose	loss
manage	management
marry	marriage
mock	mockery
move	movement
obey	obedience
obstruct	obstruction
occupy	occupation
occur	occurrence
oppose	opposition
organise	organisation
perform	performance
permit	permission
persuade	persuasion
please	pleasure
portray	portrayal
postpone	postponement
practise	practice
prepare	preparation
press	pressure
prescribe	prescription
pretend	pretence
prevail	prevalence
proceed	procedure
proclaim	proclamation

Verb	Noun
produce	production
pronounce	pronunciation
prophesy	prophecy
propose	proposal
	proposition
prosecute	prosecution
prosper	prosperity
prove	proof
provide	provision
publish	publication
punish	punishment
pursue	pursuit
qualify	qualification
rebel	rebellion
receive	receipt
recognise	recognition
reduce	reduction
relieve	relief
rely	reliance
remain	remainder
repeat	repetition
resemble	resemblance
reside	residence
resign	resignation
resist	resistance
resolve	resolution
reveal	revelation
revise	revision
revive	revival
revolve	revolution
satisfy	satisfaction
seize	seizure
serve	service
sever	severance
subscribe	subscription
succeed	success
tempt	temptation
think	thought
translate	translation
transmit	transmission

Forming Nouns

Complete each of these sentences by inserting the **noun** formed from the verb in brackets.

Example: The —— to the theatre was crowded with people. **(enter)**

Answer: **entrance**

1. The room echoed with the —— of children. **(laugh)**
2. The —— took place at St. Peter's Church. **(marry)**
3. The work of our hospitals fills us with ——. **(admire)**
4. A fierce —— ensued between the two men. **(argue)**
5. The —— of Everest was a notable feat. **(ascend)**
6. The children's —— at the concert was excellent. **(behave)**
7. The —— was led by one of the generals. **(rebel)**
8. Roy is to have a —— with the senior soccer team. **(try)**
9. The —— of the two teams was greeted by loud cheering **(appear)**
10. The —— of a long letter from home made the soldier very happy. **(receive)**

Complete each phrase by using the **noun** formed from the verb in brackets.

1. a fixed —— **(allow)**
2. a clear —— **(explain)**
3. a sound —— **(defend)**
4. thunderous —— **(applaud)**
5. an unfair —— **(compare)**
6. a public —— **(declare)**
7. by kind —— **(permit)**
8. a striking —— **(resemble)**
9. a generous —— **(subscribe)**
10. an unfortunate —— **(occur)**

Form **nouns** from these verbs.

1. perform
2. explode
3. disturb
4. arrive
5. intend
6. defy
7. divide
8. judge
9. act
10. inquire
11. move
12. depart
13. satisfy
14. prove
15. invite
16. decide
17. hate
18. grow
19. invade
20. invent

Verbs

Look at this very short sentence: **Julie cried.**

The word **cried** is an action word; it tells what Julie **did.**

Every sentence contains an action word, or words like **is, was, are, were, has, have, had, am,** etc.

Words which show action are called VERBS.

Think of the many actions you perform during the day. You **wake,** then you **rise** and **wash** and **dress** and **brush** your hair and **part** it. After **eating** your breakfast you **walk** or **ride** to school, where you **learn** to **read** good English, to **draw,** to **sing,** etc. In fact you cannot think of any time of day when you are not **doing** something. When you are tired you **rest,** and even when you **sleep** you **breathe,** and perhaps **dream** and **snore.**

EXERCISE 38

Make a list of the action words, or **verbs,** contained in the following sentences.

1. Julius Caesar invaded Britain in 55 B.C.
2. Thrushes eat worms.
3. The nightingale sings very sweetly.
4. Father put more coal on the fire.
5. The little terrier snapped at John's legs.
6. James Watt discovered the power of steam.
7. Into the Valley of Death rode the six hundred.
8. Doreen washed the dishes and wiped them.
9. Bernard took a fivepenny piece from his pocket and handed it to Anthony.
10. David likes arithmetic and enjoys every lesson.

EXERCISE 39

If you watch a football match you will see that the players perform many different kinds of actions.

Examples: trapping; heading; dribbling; kicking; shooting; jumping; charging; passing; throwing; centring, etc.

Verbs

Write the names of three **actions** performed:

1. at a cricket match
2. in a place of worship
3. in your classroom
4. by someone doing the housework.
5. on a farm
6. in a carpenter's workshop
7. by children spending a holiday at the seaside
8. by a horse in a field
9. by a needlework class
10. by a cook who is baking cakes

EXERCISE 40

Complete these sentences by fitting suitable **verbs** into the spaces.

1. When a cork is thrown into water it ——.
2. When a cat is contented it ——.
3. If sugar is put into a cup of tea it will ——.
4. During winter children sometimes —— on frozen ponds.
5. Brian —— the only goal for the school team.
6. Trespassers will be ——.
7. The motorist was —— one pound and costs.
8. Sir Francis Drake —— round the world in the *Golden Hind*.
9. Christopher Columbus —— America in 1492.
10. Smoking is —— in the new factory because it contains explosives.

EXERCISE 41

Fit these ten **verbs** into the spaces below.

| denounce | disclose | control | inherit | cancel |
| surmount | celebrate | applaud | broadcast | solve |

1. to —— a fortune
2. to —— an announcement
3. to —— a victory
4. to —— a secret
5. to —— an impostor
6. to —— a problem
7. to —— an order
8. to —— an obstacle
9. to —— one's temper
10. to —— a brilliant performance

EXERCISE 42

Insert the following verbs in the correct places in the sentences below.

awarded   **accepted**   **demolished**   **saluted**   **addressed**

performed   **committed**   **quenched**   **denied**   **skidded**

1. The soldier —— smartly as he passed the colonel.
2. Martin —— his thirst at a wayside spring.
3. The crime was —— in the early hours of the morning.
4. Both boys —— taking the bicycle away.
5. The first prize was —— to Cynthia.
6. The lorry —— on the icy road and struck a tree.
7. Julian gladly —— the offer of a lift into town.
8. As the building was unsafe it was ——.
9. A famous surgeon —— the operation on the duchess.
10. Roger —— the envelope in neat handwriting.

EXERCISE 43

Write the **verbs** indicated by the following meanings. Each asterisk (*) stands for a letter.

1. sh****   to shake with cold
2. fl*****   to praise a person more than he deserves
3. sc*****   to throw things about in various directions
4. p******e to put off to a later date
5. re*****   to turn around like a wheel
6. squ***   to look in different directions with each eye
7. *m*t*t*   to copy the actions or behaviour of someone else
8. **bble   to bite and eat small pieces of something, as mice do to cheese
9. con****   to admit having done something wrong
10. ***ish   to go out of sight

Verbs

Present Tense	Past Tense	Past Participle
am	was	been
bear	bore	borne
beat	beat	beaten
become	became	become
begin	began	begun
bite	bit	bitten
bleed	bled	bled
blow	blew	blown
break	broke	broken
bring	brought	brought
broadcast	broadcast	broadcast
build	built	built
burst	burst	burst
buy	bought	bought
catch	caught	caught
choose	chose	chosen
come	came	come
creep	crept	crept
do	did	done
draw	drew	drawn
drink	drank	drunk
deal	dealt	dealt
drive	drove	driven
drown	drowned	drowned
eat	ate	eaten
fall	fell	fallen
feel	felt	felt
fight	fought	fought
flee	fled	fled
fly	flew	flown
forget	forgot	forgotten
forsake	forsook	forsaken
freeze	froze	frozen
give	gave	given
go	went	gone
grow	grew	grown
hang (article)	hung	hung
hang (person)	hanged	hanged
hide	hid	hidden

Verbs

Present Tense	Past Tense	Past Participle
hurt	hurt	hurt
hold	held	held
kneel	knelt	knelt
know	knew	known
lay	laid	laid
leave	left	left
lie	lay	lain
mow	mowed	mown
ride	rode	ridden
ring	rang	rung
rise	rose	risen
run	ran	run
saw (wood)	sawed	sawn
see	saw	seen
seek	sought	sought
sew	sewed	sewn
shake	shook	shaken
show	showed	shown
sing	sang	sung
sink	sank	sunk
slay	slew	slain
speak	spoke	spoken
spring	sprang	sprung
steal	stole	stolen
strike	struck	struck
swear	swore	sworn
swell	swelled	swollen
swim	swam	swum
take	took	taken
teach	taught	taught
tear	tore	torn
think	thought	thought
throw	threw	thrown
tread	trod	trodden
wear	wore	worn
weave	wove	woven
wind	wound	wound
wring	wrung	wrung
write	wrote	written

Past Tense

Look at these two sentences:

    (a) The boys **know** their tables. (*Present Tense*)

    (b) The boys **knew** their tables. (*Past Tense*)

Sentence (a) tells us that the boys **know** their tables **now,** at the **present** time.

Sentence (b) tells us that the boys **knew** their tables in the **past.** What they knew then they may not know now.

The **Past Tense** of verbs can be formed in various ways.

1. The commonest method is by adding **-ed** to the Present Tense.

Examples: delight**ed**   defeat**ed**   appeal**ed**   prepar**ed**

             wonder**ed**   scream**ed**   repeat**ed**   connect**ed**

2. When the Present Tense of a verb ends with a single **e** this letter is dropped when adding **-ed.**

Examples: relate   decide   whistle   prepare

             relat**ed**   decid**ed**   whistl**ed**   prepar**ed**

EXERCISE 44

Complete each of these sentences by inserting the **Past Tense** of one of the verbs below.

refuse	**enclose**	**capture**	**receive**	**perspire**
waste	**continue**	**explore**	**describe**	**encourage**

1. The woman —— the missing coat to the policeman.
2. Brian —— a parcel by post this morning.
3. The customer —— a cheque with his order.
4. Alan's mother —— him to save for his annual holiday.
5. After the interruption the teacher —— the story.
6. Captain Cook —— the coast of Australia.
7. The police —— the bandit after a desperate struggle.
8. He —— to give his name and address.
9. The roadmen —— freely in the hot sunshine.
10. The spendthrift —— his money on useless things.

3. If the Present Tense ends with **y** this letter is changed to **i** before adding **-ed**.

Examples:

rely	defy	terrify	multiply
rel**ied**	def**ied**	terrif**ied**	multipl**ied**

EXERCISE 45

Use the **Past Tense** of these verbs to fill the spaces.

study	deny	bury	apply	hurry
occupy	reply	supply	copy	satisfy

1. He —— to school because he thought it was late.
2. The school cooks —— all the cakes for the party.
3. The poodle —— the best chair in the lounge.
4. Bill —— two of the sums from Desmond.
5. He —— having done so.
6. Geoffrey —— his curiosity by peeping through the window.
7. The terrier —— his bone in the garden.
8. Most pupils —— the questions well before answering them.
9. The clerk —— for an increase in salary.
10. Mary —— to Jean's invitation by return of post.

4. Many verbs form their Past Tense by doubling the final letter of the Present Tense before adding **-ed**.

Examples:

drop	plan	beg	rob	expel
drop**ped**	plan**ned**	beg**ged**	rob**bed**	expel**led**

EXERCISE 46

Fill in the spaces below with the **Past Tense** of these verbs.

stir	compel	prefer	travel	pin
drip	skid	knit	stop	occur

1. Judith —— a cardigan for her little sister.
2. The slow train to Liverpool —— at every station.
3. Jane —— the two pieces of material together.
4. The car —— on the icy road and overturned.
5. Several children —— to school by bus.
6. Many accidents in the home —— last year.
7. Water —— from Martin's raincoat on to the floor.
8. Sandra —— her tea before drinking it.
9. The boxer —— his opponent to retire.
10. The boys said that they —— playing football to cricket.

Past Tense

5. The Past Tense of many verbs is formed **not** by adding **-ed,** but by changing one or more letters.

Examples: ring   write   wake   swim   tear

               rang   wrote   woke   swam   tore

EXERCISE 47

Complete these sentences by using the **Past Tense** of the verbs given at the end. These are **not** formed by adding **-ed.**

1. Richard —— the school bell. (**ring**)
2. The girl did not reply when I —— to her. (**speak**)
3. Two boys —— from Brighton to London on their cycles. (**ride**)
4. The maid —— the wet clothes and put them before the fire. (**wring**)
5. Gerald —— a cricket bat for a birthday present. (**choose**)
6. Margaret —— a fine picture of the school. (**draw**)
7. It was so cold that the water in the pond ——. (**freeze**)
8. The boys —— their work thoroughly. (**do**)
9. With a snarl the tiger —— at the bullock. (**spring**)
10. The instructor —— me the breast stroke. (**teach**)
11. James —— all his sweets. (**eat**)
12. Tony blew the balloon up so high that it ——. (**burst**)
13. The batsman —— his hand and had to retire. (**hurt**)
14. Charles —— Ronald in the English test. (**beat**)
15. The chairman —— from his seat to give his report. (**rise**)
16. Philip —— his football to school today. (**bring**)
17. We —— many interesting things in the museum. (**see**)
18. The injured man —— the pain in silence. (**bear**)
19. The defeated army —— from the battlefield. (**flee**)
20. St. George —— the dragon. (**slay**)

EXERCISE 48

Rewrite this paragraph, changing all the verbs in **heavy type** from the **Present Tense** to the **Past Tense.**

On the day of the picnic I **rise** early, **choose** a shirt with an open neck, **bring** it downstairs and **begin** getting ready. During breakfast I **bite** my tongue and **hurt** it, so I **catch** hold of a mug of hot milk and **drink** some, but the mug **falls** to the floor and **breaks.**

40

EXERCISE 49

Change all the verbs in these sentences from the **Past Tense** to the **Present Tense.**

Example: Carol **went** to the ball and **wore** her new dress.

Answer: Carol **goes** to the ball and **wears** her new dress.

1. Harold sat on the settee and began to read his new book.
2. Jean told her mother that Hazel kept rabbits.
3. As the children grew they learnt to read and write.
4. After the race Paul felt tired and went to bed.
5. With a grunt Robin tore up the letter he wrote.
6. As the clock struck twelve Cinderella ran from the ballroom.
7. Tired out, Father sank into an armchair and slept for nearly three hours.
8. The hunted man knew that he was cornered and gave himself up.
9. The shopkeeper sold his goods and paid his creditors.
10. Jane crept upstairs and lay on the bed.

EXERCISE 50

Write the correct form of the verb in the spaces below.

Today	Yesterday		Today	Yesterday
1. I wake	I woke		11. I hide	I ——
2. I dig	I ——		12. I leave	I ——
3. I bend	I ——		13. I swim	I ——
4. I bury	I ——		14. I sing	I ——
5. I beat	I ——		15. I say	I ——
6. I fly	I ——		16. I blow	I ——
7. I meet	I ——		17. I tear	I ——
8. I bleed	I ——		18. I become	I ——
9. I am	I ——		19. I build	I ——
10. I come	I ——		20. I drive	I ——

Past Tense

Insert in each sentence below the **Past Tense** of the verb at the end. In every case the Past Tense is formed by adding **-ed,** but remember the spelling rules.

1. Bill —— at the top of his voice. (**shout**)
2. Conditions on the Bounty were so bad that the crew ——. (**mutiny**)
3. We all —— Peter's new bicycle. (**admire**)
4. The cup-tie —— a crowd of fifty thousand. (**attract**)
5. The navvies —— the earth back into the trench. (**shovel**)
6. John Charles —— the ball cleverly. (**trap**)
7. Mr. Thompson —— that my work was improving. (**remark**)
8. The school garden —— fine vegetables this year. (**produce**)
9. A helmet —— the fireman's head. (**protect**)
10. Joseph —— that there would be a seven years' famine in Egypt. (**prophesy**)
11. Carlo —— his bone in the seed-bed. (**bury**)
12. The police —— the prisoner to smoke. (**permit**)
13. Twenty-six policemen —— the traffic. (**control**)
14. We —— that the river was rising quickly. (**notice**)
15. The weather was so bad that we —— the match. (**cancel**)
16. Mother —— this pullover for me. (**knit**)
17. June —— the lounge for her mother. (**tidy**)
18. The dog —— the rabbit right into the wood. (**pursue**)
19. The boys —— over their game. (**quarrel**)
20. Jean —— the dishes and broke them. (**drop**)

Insert in each space below the **Past Tense** of the verb in brackets.

1. Father —— the clock. (**wind**)
2. Dickens —— Oliver Twist. (**write**)
3. The clock —— twelve. (**strike**)
4. Mother —— me ten pence. (**give**)
5. The patient —— better. (**feel**)
6. Ann —— the baby. (**hold**)
7. Arthur —— he was lost. (**think**)
8. Janice —— those flowers. (**grow**)
9. They —— like Trojans. (**fight**)
10. The leaking boat soon ——. (**sank**)

Past Tense

Write the **Past Tense** of each of the following verbs.

1. cut	6. broadcast	11. wear	16. find
2. drink	7. steal	12. trend	17. forsake
3. forget	8. deal	13. dread	18. dream
4. throw	9. leap	14. drown	19. kneel
5. take	10. shake	15. swear	20. smell

Points to Remember

Mistakes are often made when using the Past Tense of certain verbs. Look at these examples.

Wrong: The mason **hurted** his hand at work.
Right: The mason **hurt** his hand at work.

Wrong: I **done** it all by myself.
Right: I **did** it all by myself.

Wrong: I **seen** him with my own eyes.
Right: I **saw** him with my own eyes.

Wrong: Jack **rose** his hat to Mrs. Wilkins.
Right: Jack **raised** his hat to Mrs. Wilkins.

Wrong: They **drownded** the unwanted kittens.
Right: They **drowned** the unwanted kittens.

Wrong: I **give** him my answer last week.
Right: I **gave** him my answer last week.

Wrong: He **lays** in bed till ten o'clock.
Right: He **lies** in bed till ten o'clock.

Participles

Look at these two sentences:

> (a) The bulldog **bit** Tom.
>
> (b) Tom **was bitten** by the bulldog.

In (a) the word **bit** is the **Past Tense** of **bite.**

In (b) the word **bitten** is the **Past Participle** of **bite.**

Notice that **the Participle needs a helping word,** such as

> was were has have had

The Past Tense requires no helping word.

EXERCISE 54

Complete each of these sentences by inserting the **Past Participle** of the verb in brackets. Underline the helping word in each sentence.

Example: The puppy <u>was</u> given to the boy at Christmas.

1. When the carpet was —— there were clouds of dust. **(beat)**
2. Some children arrived after the first lesson had ——. **(begin)**
3. Thousands of tubs of ice-cream were —— last summer. **(eat)**
4. Much valuable work is —— by voluntary helpers. **(do)**
5. Several windows were —— by the violent gale. **(break)**
6. In the excitement the cooking was quite ——. **(forget)**
7. The pipe was ——, so we could get not water. **(freeze)**
8. Betty was —— to be Carnival Queen this year. **(choose)**
9. Huge quantities of lemonade were —— at the children's party. **(drink)**
10. Burglars had —— the week's takings. **(steal)**
11. The tramp's boots were —— through. **(wear)**
12. The school bell was —— at 9 o'clock. **(ring)**
13. Those pictures were —— by Esme. **(draw)**
14. The two girls have not —— to each other since they quarrelled. **(speak)**
15. Jack was —— by the farmer's dog. **(bite)**
16. The jet liner had —— the Atlantic in record time. **(fly)**
17. Some of our best-known novels were —— by Charles Dickens. **(write)**
18. As the clouds gathered the sun was —— from view. **(hide)**
19. After the leaves had —— from the trees the countryside looked quite bare. **(fall)**
20. The house was —— by the explosion. **(shake)**

Participles

(a) A cobra **bit** the hunter in the leg. (*Past Tense*)

(b) The hunter **was bitten** in the leg by a cobra. (*Participle*)

Notice how the order of the words has been changed, also that a different form of the verb **bite** is used.

Now do the same with these sentences.

1. Father grew those lovely roses.
2. The police knew the leader of the gang.
3. Stirling Moss drove the winning car.
4. Robert blew the football up.
5. Two men laid the new carpet.
6. The choir sang several choruses.
7. The gardener mowed the lawns.
8. Barbed wire tore Gerald's coat.
9. St. George slew the dragon.
10. A soldier saw the escaped convict.

EXERCISE 56

Fill in each space with the correct form of the verb given.

1. **take**   the money was ——
2. **give**   the book was ——
3. **throw**   the stone was ——
4. **tread**   it was —— on
5. **swim**   the Channel was ——
6. **sew**   the shoe was ——
7. **wind**   the clock was ——
8. **run**   the race was ——
9. **hold**   the wood was ——
10. **catch**   the trout was ——
11. **swear**   an oath was ——
12. **forsake** the beach was ——
13. **spring**   a surprise was ——
14. **show**   films were ——
15. **drown**   the sailor was ——
16. **burst**   the tyre was ——
17. **bear**   the pain was ——
18. **sink**   the ship was ——
19. **weave**   the cloth was ——
20. **hang**   the curtains were ——

Adjectives

Both in writing and speaking we must make our thoughts as clear as possible.

If the police are seeking a criminal they are given a description of him.

If they are told that he is a **tall** man they need not consider any **short** men.

Again, if they know that he is **broad** they can rule out all **tall, thin** men as well as all **short** men.

As we add words to describe the wanted man the field of search becomes smaller, so you see how useful these describing words are.

A word which describes a noun is called an ADJECTIVE.

EXERCISE 57

Make a list of the **describing words,** or **adjectives,** found in the following sentences.

1. The weather was sunny but cold.
2. The large crowd saw a thrilling match.
3. A hungry man is an angry man.
4. The old woman was very proud of her new house.
5. The ancient mariner raised his skinny hand.
6. Fine feathers make fine birds.
7. The first batsman was out to a brilliant catch by Evans.
8. A black, shaggy dog barked furiously at the visitors.
9. Sheila wore a rough, woollen cardigan.
10. The explorers were tired and disheartened.

In describing something we often have several adjectives to choose from.

For example: **fruit** may be **ripe, juicy, sour, sweet, bitter, dry, tempting, rotten, delicious, luscious, appetising,** etc.

Adjectives

EXERCISE 58

Write these ten nouns in a column at the left side of the page. After each write three **adjectives** which may be used to describe it.

Example: story   interesting; thrilling; humorous

Noun	Adjectives		
1. game	....	....	....
2. work	....	....	....
3. sea	....	....	....
4. dress	....	....	....
5. flower	....	....	....
6. house	....	....	....
7. weather	....	....	....
8. voice	....	....	....
9. dog	....	....	....
10. food	....	....	....

EXERCISE 59

Write the ten **adjectives** below in a column as shown, then opposite each write the noun which matches it.

Example: **1. prosperous business**

Adjectives	Nouns
1. prosperous	lane
2. loyal	flower
3. celebrated	weather
4. rusty	clouds
5. muddy	subjects
6. fragrant	injuries
7. delicious	business
8. fleecy	pianist
9. changeable	railings
10. severe	pastries

47

Comparing Adjectives

Robin
tall

Duncan
taller

Bruce
tallest

(a) Robin is a **tall** boy, measuring 154 centimetres at the age of eleven.
(b) Duncan is 160 centimetres in height, so he is 6 centimetres **taller** than Robin.
(c) Bruce is 165 centimetres tall, so he is the **tallest** of the three boys.

In (a) we considered only **one** boy. No comparison was made so we used the adjective **tall.**

This is called the POSITIVE DEGREE.

In (b) we compared the height of Duncan with that of one other boy, Robin, so we used the word **taller.**

When we compare **two** persons or things we use the COMPARATIVE DEGREE.

In (c) we compared Bruce with **more than one** other boy by saying that he is the **tallest** of the three.

In comparing **more than two** persons or things we use the SUPERLATIVE DEGREE.

You will notice that a simple way of comparing adjectives is to:

add **-er** for the Comparative Degree, and to

add **-est** for the Superlative Degree.

Many adjectives have the **-er** and **-est** added without any change in spelling.

Examples:

small	smaller	smallest
bright	brighter	brightest
smooth	smoother	smoothest
narrow	narrower	narrowest

If the adjective ends with **e** this letter is dropped when adding **-er** or **-est.**

48

Comparing Adjectives

Examples:

large	larger	largest
brave	braver	bravest
wise	wiser	wisest
safe	safer	safest
pale	paler	palest

When the adjective ends with **-y** this letter is changed to **-i** before adding **-er** or **-est**.

Examples:

heavy	heavier	heaviest
busy	busier	busiest
healthy	healthier	healthiest
noisy	noisier	noisiest
lucky	luckier	luckiest

In the case of certain adjectives the last letter is doubled before adding **-er** or **-est**.

Examples:

thin	thinner	thinnest
hot	hotter	hottest
big	bigger	biggest
fat	fatter	fattest
red	redder	reddest

Adjectives of three syllables, and some of two syllables, have **more** written before them for the Comparative Degree, and **most** for the Superlative Degree.

Examples:

beautiful	more beautiful	most beautiful
delicious	more delicious	most delicious
humorous	more humorous	most humorous
honest	more honest	most honest
efficient	more efficient	most efficient

Some adjectives are irregular, and it is these which cause most trouble in writing and speaking English.

Examples:

good	better	best
bad	worse	worst
little	less	least
many	more	most
much	more	most

49

Comparing Adjectives

Complete these sentences by inserting the correct degree of the adjective in brackets.

1. This is the —— book in the library. (**thin**)
2. The church is the —— building in the county. (**old**)
3. Frances occupied the —— chair in the lounge. (**comfortable**)
4. Today's weather is —— than yesterday's. (**bad**)
5. Weather reports say it is the —— we have had for nine years. (**bad**)
6. Sir James is —— than his brother. (**generous**)
7. Sir Winston Churchill was the —— Englishman in World War II. (**famous**)
8. The hotel manager was the —— we had ever met. (**polite**)
9. The farmer said this was the —— of the two turkeys. (**fat**)
10. Undoubtedly this is the —— of the two tennis rackets. (**good**)
11. Pamela is the —— girl in the class. (**brilliant**)
12. When the two boxers weighed in Cooper was the —— by one kilogram. (**heavy**)
13. Colin was the —— dancer in the ballroom. (**graceful**)
14. Both exercises are **difficult** but the second is the —— of the two.
15. This is the —— idea of the year. (**original**)
16. Enid is the —— of the Robinson twins. (**pretty**)
17. The cottage on the moor was the —— ever built. (**crude**)
18. Both Mr. and Mrs. Davies have a car, but his is the ——. (**powerful**)
19. The boy chose the cakes which looked the ——. (**sweet**)
20. There are two roads leading to the village, the lower road being the —— one. (**narrow**)

Comparing Adjectives

1. Write six adjectives which form their comparisons by adding
   -er and **-est** without change of spelling, then compare them.

   Example: **long   longer   longest**

2. Write the Comparative Degree of six adjectives ending with
   -er from which the **-e** is dropped in adding **-er.**

   Example: **strange   stranger**

3. Write the Superlative Degree of six adjectives ending with **-y**
   in which this letter is changed to **-i** before adding **-est.**

   Example: **cosy   cosiest**

4. Give six adjectives which are compared by adding **more** and
   most. Then write all three degrees.

   Example: **cautious   more cautious   most cautious**

5. Write the Comparative Degree of six adjectives in which the
   last letter is doubled before adding **-er.**

   Example: **sad   sadder**

Compare the following adjectives.

1. clever	11. wide
2. rude	12. cold
3. noisy	13. bad
4. jealous	14. sturdy
5. patient	15. splendid
6. wealthy	16. dirty
7. little	17. faithful
8. gracious	18. ignorant
9. industrious	19. thin
10. good	20. plucky

Comparing Adjectives

What to Avoid in Using Adjectives

1. Avoid using the **Superlative Degree** when the **Comparative Degree** is required.

   Wrong: This book is the **best** of the two.

   Right: This book is the **better** of the two.

2. Do not use **less** instead of **fewer.**

   Wrong: Ann made **less** mistakes than Diana.

   Right: Ann made **fewer** mistakes than Diana.

   Remember that **less** is used for a **quantity,** e.g. **less** butter; **less** fruit; etc.

   Fewer is used for **numbers of things,** e.g. **fewer** cows; **fewer** parties; etc.

3. Avoid using **worse** for **worst.**

   Wrong: Brenda is the **worse** writer in the class.

   Right: Brenda is the **worst** writer in the class.

4. Avoid using **more** with an adjective which forms its Comparative Degree by adding **-er.**

   Wrong: It is **more cheaper** to travel by road.

   Right: It is **cheaper** to travel by road.

5. Use **elder** and **eldest** for persons, usually those of the same family.

   Examples: Mr. Payne's **elder** daughter is engaged. (two daughters)

   May is Mr. Benn's **eldest** daughter. (more than two)

6. **Older** and **oldest** are used for things and unrelated persons.

   Examples: This is the **oldest** castle in the country.

   George is the **oldest** inhabitant in the village.

Forming Adjectives

Adjectives Formed from Nouns

Noun	Adjective	Noun	Adjective
accident	accidental	expression	expressive
advantage	advantageous	fable	fabulous
adventure	adventurous	faith	{ faithful / faithless
affection	affectionate	fame	famous
ancestor	ancestral	fashion	fashionable
angel	angelic	fault	faulty
anger	angry	favour	favourite
anxiety	anxious	fire	fiery
athlete	athletic	five	fifth
autumn	autumnal	fool	{ foolish / foolhardy
beauty	{ beautiful / beauteous	fortune	fortunate
bible	biblical	fraud	fraudulent
boy	boyish	friend	{ friendly / friendless
capacity	capacious	fur	furry
caution	cautious	fury	furious
centre	central	giant	gigantic
charity	charitable	girl	girlish
child	childish	gold	golden
choir	choral	grace	graceful
circle	circular	grief	grievous
colony	colonial	haste	hasty
comfort	comfortable	hero	heroic
continent	continental	humour	humorous
courage	courageous	hygiene	hygienic
coward	cowardly	industry	{ industrial / industrious
craft	crafty	influence	influential
credit	creditable	injury	injurious
crime	criminal	labour	laborious
custom	customary	luxury	luxurious
danger	dangerous	man	manly
deceit	deceitful	marvel	marvellous
disaster	disastrous	melody	melodious
economy	economical	metal	metallic
effect	effective		
energy	energetic		
expense	expensive		

53

Forming Adjectives

Adjectives Formed from Nouns

Noun	Adjective	Noun	Adjective
mercy	merciful	response	⎰ responsive / responsible
method	methodical	school	scholastic
miracle	miraculous	sense	⎰ sensible / senseless
mischief	mischievous		
misery	miserable	service	serviceable
mountain	mountainous	shower	showery
muscle	muscular	skill	skilful
music	musical	squalor	squalid
mystery	mysterious	star	starry
nation	national	sun	sunny
nature	natural	suspicion	suspicious
noise	⎰ noisy / noiseless	sympathy	sympathetic
nonsense	nonsensical	tempest	tempestuous
occasion	occasional	terror	⎰ terrible / terror-stricken
ocean	oceanic		
ornament	ornamental	triangle	triangular
peril	perilous	tribe	tribal
person	personal	value	valuable
picture	picturesque	victory	victorious
pirate	piratical	vigour	vigorous
poet	⎰ poetic / poetical	volcano	volcanic
		water	watery
poison	poisonous	winter	wintry
rebellion	rebellious	wool	woollen
region	regional	wretch	wretched

Forming Adjectives

Complete each sentence by inserting the **adjective** formed from the noun in **heavy type.**

Example: **service**   This has been a very —— raincoat.

Answer: This has been a very **serviceable** raincoat.

1. **centre**   The shop was situated in a —— position.
2. **luxury**   The new liner has the most —— cabins.
3. **value**   Gold is a very —— metal.
4. **mischief**   The —— boys trampled on the flower-beds.
5. **energy**   He feels quite —— after his holiday abroad.
6. **athlete**   The runner was a man of —— build.
7. **star**   We studied the —— sky through a telescope.
8. **humour**   Mark Twain wrote many —— stories.
9. **angel**   The choirboy had a most —— face.
10. **friend**   A —— person soon puts you at your ease.

Complete these phrases, using the **adjectives** formed from the nouns at the end.

1. a —— sea (**tempest**)
2. —— berries (**poison**)
3. a —— cure (**miracle**)
4. a —— suggestion (**sense**)
5. a —— sound (**metal**)
6. an —— friend (**influence**)
7. an —— home (**ancestor**)
8. an —— discovery (**accident**)
9. an —— town (**industry**)
10. an —— outing (**expense**)

Form **adjectives** from the following nouns.

1. misery
2. caution
3. courage
4. favour
5. skill
6. disaster
7. anger
8. grief
9. picture
10. fable
11. fortune
12. nature
13. vigour
14. circle
15. method
16. crime
17. sympathy
18. fury
19. custom
20. winter

Proper Adjectives

Proper Noun	Proper Adjective	Proper Noun	Proper Adjective
Alps	Alpine	Israel	Israeli
Belgium	Belgian	Italy	Italian
Brazil	Brazilian	Japan	Japanese
Britain	British	Malta	Maltese
Canada	Canadian	Mexico	Mexican
China	Chinese	Naples	Neapolitan
Cyprus	Cypriot	Norway	Norwegian
Czechoslovakia	Czech	Pakistan	Pakistani
Denmark	Danish	Paris	Parisian
Egypt	Egyptian	Persia	Persian
Europe	European	Poland	Polish
Finland	Finnish	Portugal	Portuguese
France	French	Scotland	Scottish
Genoa	Genoese	Siam	Siamese
Germany	German	Sicily	Sicilian
Ghana	Ghanaian	Spain	Spanish
Greece	Greek	Sweden	Swedish
Holland	Dutch	Switzerland	Swiss
Hungary	Hungarian	Tibet	Tibetan
Iceland	Icelandic	Turkey	Turkish
Iraq	Iraqi	Venice	Venetian
Ireland	Irish	Vienna	Viennese
Isle of Man	Manx	Wales	Welsh

EXERCISE 66

Insert the correct **proper adjective** in each phrase below.

1. —— twins (**Siam**)
2. —— lamb (**Persia**)
3. —— fashions (**Paris**)
4. —— climbers (**Alps**)
5. —— canals (**Venice**)
6. —— oranges (**Israel**)
7. —— dances (**Vienna**)
8. —— monks (**Tibet**)
9. —— athletes (**Finland**)
10. —— trawlers (**Iceland**)

Proper Adjectives

Rewrite these sentences, using the correct **proper adjective.**

1. The —— Riviera is noted for its warm climate. (**France**)
2. Drake sailed to fight the —— Armada. (**Spain**)
3. Large quantities of —— butter are imported into Britain every year. (**Denmark**)
4. A ship laden with —— timber reached London yesterday. (**Sweden**)
5. I pulled up the —— blinds. (**Venice**)
6. We plant —— bulbs in our garden. (**Holland**)
7. We lunched at an —— restaurant. (**Italy**)
8. The tour included a visit to several —— fiords. (**Norway**)
9. Roger is spending a holiday on the —— coast. (**Belgium**)
10. Most —— cattle ranches are very large. (**Canada**)

In each space insert the **adjective** formed from the Proper Noun.

1. The humour of Ireland   —— humour
2. The lakes of Switzerland   the —— lakes
3. The people of Egypt   the —— people
4. A village in Mexico   a —— village
5. The King of Denmark   the —— King
6. Chocolates from Belgium   —— chocolates
7. Wine from Portugal   —— wine
8. The Highlands of Scotland   the —— Highlands
9. The population of Malta   the —— population
10. A cat from the Isle of Man   a —— cat

Form **proper adjectives** from:

1. Hungary	6. Pakistan	11. Naples
2. Britain	7. Europe	12. Japan
3. Turkey	8. Cyprus	13. Genoa
4. Brazil	9. Iraq	14. Czechoslovakia
5. Sicily	10. Ghana	15. Portugal

Adverbs

Read this sentence carefully.

Bill walked **slowly** down the street.

The word **slowly** tells us how Bill walked.

He could have walked in several different ways, each of which could be described by one word.

Examples: **briskly; hurriedly; leisurely; lamely; quickly; smartly; joyfully;** etc.

> Words which describe how actions are done are called ADVERBS.

Adverbs may tell us how, when or where an action is done, but we shall consider only the **how** words.

EXERCISE 70

Pick out the **adverbs** in these sentences and write them down. Then use them in sentences of your own.

1. The puppy ate his food greedily.
2. Grandpa laughed heartily at his own joke.
3. The champion boxed cleverly in the closing rounds.
4. The choir sang sweetly at the concert.
5. Marjorie gazed thoughtfully at the fire.
6. We worked our sums easily.
7. The Persian cat looked hungrily at the white mice.
8. The duchess left the room hurriedly.
9. Grandma was seated comfortably in the armchair.
10. The bulldog growled fiercely at the tramp.

You will notice that all the adverbs in these sentences end with **-ly,** though some adverbs do not. *Example:* The doctor did his work **well.**

Adverbs can be formed from adjectives by adding **-ly,** but spelling changes are often necessary.

Adverbs

No change	Change y to i	Drop e	No change
cleverly	heartily	humbly	gratefully
sweetly	hungrily	nobly	thankfully
quickly	angrily	sensibly	hopefully
cheaply	noisily	gently	carefully
plainly	luckily	simply	truthfully
distinctly	steadily	miserably	skilfully
suddenly	shabbily	comfortably	mentally
poorly	wearily	idly	accidentally
fairly	heavily	horribly	brutally
proudly	clumsily	feebly	equally
bravely	merrily	possibly	loyally
anxiously	easily	truly	annually
gladly	haughtily	suitably	scornfully
patiently	lazily	terribly	fatally
willingly	prettily	probably	practically

Note that the l is not dropped when -ly is added to adjectives ending with -ful.

EXERCISE 71

Write these ten verbs in a column, and opposite each write three adverbs to describe **how** the action is done.

Example: **walking:** hurriedly   leisurely   unsteadily

1. eating   ....
2. fighting   ....
3. laughing   ....
4. working   ....
5. dancing   ....
6. boxing   ....
7. talking   ....
8. running   ....
9. reading   ....
10. sleeping   ....

Adverbs

EXERCISE 72

gratefully   **reverently**   **respectfully**   **longingly**   **attentively**

gracefully   **loyally**   **thoroughly**   **heatedly**   **proudly**

From the **adverbs** above select the one which best tells:

1. How a swan swims.
2. How people often speak in an argument.
3. How we should accept gifts.
4. How a hungry dog looks at a meaty bone which he cannot reach.
5. How a parent speaks of a successful son or daughter.
6. How pupils should listen to a lesson.
7. How we should behave in a place of worship.
8. How often employees speak to their employers.
9. How we should do our work.
10. How friends often stick up for each other.

EXERCISE 73

Write the ten **verbs** below in a column, as shown, then write after each the **adverb** in the second column which matches it.

Verbs	**Adverbs**
1. fought	aimlessly
2. listened	faithfully
3. paused	awkwardly
4. waited	fluently
5. gave	punctually
6. spoke	patiently
7. promised	intently
8. fell	heroically
9. wandered	generously
10. arrived	momentarily

EXERCISE 74

Form **adverbs** from these adjectives, then use each in a sentence of your own.

1. polite	4. sad	7. strong	10. kind
2. careless	5. cautious	8. frequent	11. fatal
3. bitter	6. suitable	9. abrupt	12. prompt

Adverbs

Complete each sentence below by inserting one of these adverbs.

breathlessly **comfortably** **rapidly** **skilfully** **correctly**

fearlessly **frantically** **angrily** **stealthily** **immediately**

1. The boys crept —— from the room.
2. The survivors on the raft waved —— to the passing liner.
3. The workmen protested —— against their working conditions.
4. Sylvia answered every question ——.
5. Grandpa was seated —— in his big armchair.
6. The crowd watched —— as the fireman entered the blazing building.
7. On hearing the news the doctor went to the house ——.
8. The fog spread —— over the whole countryside.
9. With his rifle ready the hunter faced the lion ——.
10. The carving on the oak panels has been —— done.

In each sentence below certain words are in heavy type. Rewrite each sentence, using an **adverb** in place of these words.

Example: The prisoner was beaten **without mercy.**

Answer: The prisoner was beaten **unmercifully.**

1. The speaker left the room **in a hurry.**
2. Norman jumped 1½ metres **with ease.**
3. The child was sleeping **in peace.**
4. We can look forward to the future **with hope.**
5. The Chinese vase was broken **by accident.**
6. The little boy's head was nodding **with sleep.**
7. The tramp looked **with scorn** at the crust the lady gave him.
8. Derek worked all the sums **in his head.**
9. The gardener gazed **with pride** at his lovely roses.
10. Although outnumbered the troops fought **like heroes.**

Pronouns

Read this sentence:

John hit out at the ball, but John missed the ball and James stumped John.

Notice that you are told **three** things about John.

(a) John hit out at the ball.

(b) John missed the ball.

(c) James stumped John.

The word **John** occurs **three** times. Now read this sentence:

John hit out at the ball, but he missed it and James stumped him.

The word **he** is used in place of **John** the second time, and the word **him** the third time. Also, the word **it** is used in place of the noun **ball.**

> A word which takes the place of a noun is called a PRONOUN.

Here are some pronouns commonly used:

I	**we**	**me**	**us**
you	**you**	**you**	**you**
he, she, it	**they**	**him, her, it**	**them**

These pronouns show possession:

mine	**ours**
yours	**yours**
his, hers, its	**theirs**

Remember that	Remember that
its	**it's**
means 'belonging to it'	means 'it is'

Note: Possessive pronouns do not use the apostrophe. The apostrophe is used in **it's,** meaning **it is,** because the letter **i** has been dropped from **is.**

EXERCISE 77

Rewrite these sentences, using **pronouns** where necessary to avoid repeating the nouns.

1. The pilot said that the pilot had made a forced landing.
2. The children cried when the children were scolded.
3. Dorothy's mother asked Dorothy to dust the lounge.
4. The captain told the crew that the captain wanted to speak to the crew when the ship docked.
5. The queen said that the queen had a severe headache.
6. The sister ordered the nurses to report to the sister when the nurses went off duty.
7. Judith said that Judith would be meeting a friend of Judith's.
8. Robin took one look at the gun and saw that the gun was Robin's.
9. The surgeon told Mrs. Cook that the surgeon would operate on Mrs. Cook immediately.
10. The police informed the jeweller that the police had arrested the man who had robbed the jeweller.

EXERCISE 78

Write the following sentences in a shorter form by using **possessive pronouns**.

Example: This pen belongs to **me**. This pen is **mine**.

1. This pistol belongs to him. This pistol is ——.
2. Does the blue scarf belong to her? Is the blue scarf ——?
3. You must take responsibility. The responsibility is ——.
4. This bell tent belongs to us. The bell tent is ——.
5. This model aeroplane belongs to me. This model aeroplane is ——.
6. The new caravan belongs to them. The new caravan is ——.

Using the Correct Pronoun

The pronouns **I** and **me** cause much confusion, so it is important to know how to use them properly. Would you use **I** or **me** in this sentence?

Keith and —— are going to the cinema.

If you are in doubt you should divide the sentence into two short sentences, like this:

Keith is going to the cinema. I am going to the cinema.

You could not possibly say, "**Me** am going to the cinema."

Pronouns

Consider this sentence:

Father told Rupert and —— to wait for him.

Make two sentences: Father told Rupert to wait for him.

Father told —— to wait for him.

You could not say, "Father told **I** to wait for him."

The correct form is: Father told Rupert and **me** to wait for him.

Note: **Me** is always used after **between.**

Wrong: It is a secret between Jane and **I.**

Right: It is a secret between Jane and **me.**

EXERCISE 79

Fill in the correct **pronoun** in each sentence below, using the rules you have just learnt.

1. Francis and —— are going to the party.
2. Brian invited Paul and —— to his party.
3. Between you and —— the grocer is short of money.
4. Richard and —— received presents from Uncle David.
5. Uncle David sent presents for Richard and ——.
6. Mother scolded Janet and —— for being late.
7. Aunt Muriel said that Bob and —— were to share this chocolate.
8. Aunt Muriel said that this chocolate was to be shared between Bob and ——.
9. There was trouble in store for Sally and ——.
10. It was evident that Sally and —— were in trouble.

Connecting Words

Read these two sentences: Robert was very hungry.

Alan was very hungry.

We can link these sentences by saying: Robert **and** Alan were very hungry.

The word **and** is used to join together the words Robert and Alan, and is called a CONJUNCTION. (Think of a railway junction, where one railway **joins** another.)

Now consider these sentences: The girls walked down the road.

The girls turned into the park.

We can join these two statements to make one sentence:

The girls walked down the road **and** turned into the park.

In this case the conjunction **and** joins **two groups of words.**

A CONJUNCTION is a word which joins together two single words or two groups of words.

Here are some **conjunctions** which are in everyday use.

if	for	since	unless
as	yet	while	because
and	that	until	whether
but	when	though	although

EXERCISE 80

Use one of the **conjunctions** in the list above to complete each of these sentences.

1. Mother paid the butcher —— put the meat in her basket.
2. The wind was cold —— it was the month of March.
3. Brian did not know —— to choose a cricket bat or a football for a birthday present.
4. Let us sit on the beach —— the sun sets, then go indoors and change.
5. Susan boiled the eggs —— Jane cut the bread-and-butter.

Connecting Words

6. You need not come with us —— you wish to.
7. We intend going to Eastbourne —— the weather is fine.
8. Bernard burnt his fingers —— he had been warned to be careful with the fireworks.
9. The match was postponed —— of the heavy rain.
10. We looked everywhere for the lost book —— could not find it.

Other Words Used as Connecting Words

Look at these sentences: This is the house.

Jack built it.

We can join these: This is the house **that** Jack built.

The word **that** refers to the house, and is therefore a **pronoun,** but it also does the work of a **conjunction.**

Take another example: We saw the Boy Scout.

He saved a girl from drowning.

One sentence: We saw the Boy Scout **who** saved a girl from drowning.

The connecting word in this sentence is **who.**

Remember: We use **who** in referring to persons.

Example: The crowd cheered the competitors **who** were walking from John o'Groat's to Land's End.

We use **which** for animals and things.

Examples: (a) We had an interesting lesson on the camel, **which** is sometimes called 'the ship of the desert'. (*animal*)
(b) At the dance Alice wore the beautiful frock **which** the Duchess had given her. (*thing*)

We use **that** for persons, animals and things.

Examples: (a) The convict **that** escaped has been recaptured. (*person*)
(b) The stray dog **that** killed the sheep was shot by the farmer. (*animal*)
(c) I cannot find the book **that** I promised to lend you. (*thing*)

66

Connecting Words

In addition to **who,** the words **whom** and **whose** are also used to refer to persons.

Examples: Charles is a conceited boy. I dislike him very much.

Charles is a conceited boy **whom** I dislike very much.

We met a Frenchman. His name was Pierre.

We met a Frenchman **whose** name was Pierre.

EXERCISE 81

Below are pairs of sentences. Join them together by using **who, whose, whom, that** or **which.**

1. Handel was a famous composer. He wrote some of the world's greatest music.

2. At the museum we saw a sword. It had belonged to Lord Nelson.

3. I have just sold the book. I bought it yesterday.

4. There is the policeman. To him I gave the watch I found.

5. At the police station there was a man. His house had just been burgled.

6. A large crowd watched the steeplejack. He was seated on top of the church tower.

7. We saw the jet fighter. It crashed in a field behind our house yesterday.

8. Next door to us lives a German boy. His father is a circus acrobat.

9. Jean resembles her mother. From her she gets her good looks.

10. The clerk was robbed of a suitcase. It contained the wages of the staff.

11. I am sure this is the film. Jane told us about it.

12. The police took charge of the little child. It had lost its way.

Prepositions

Look at these pictures.

In (a) the boy is sitting **on** the table.

In (b) he is hiding **under** the table.

In (c) he is leaning **against** the table.

In (d) he is standing **by** the table.

The words in heavy type show the relationship between the boy and the table.

> A word which shows the relationship between a noun, or pronoun, and another word in a sentence is called a PREPOSITION.

Here is a list of **prepositions** in common use.

aboard	behind	from	through
about	below	in	till
above	beneath	into	to
across	beside	near	towards
after	between	of	under
against	beyond	off	until
along	by	on	up
among	down	opposite	upon
around	during	over	with
at	except	past	within
before	for	since	without

Using Prepositions Correctly

1. among   Something is shared among **several** persons.
   between   Something is shared between **two** persons.

Prepositions

2. beside	This means **at the side of.** (The doctor stood **beside** the bed.)
besides	This means **in addition to.** (Several girls were there **besides** Margaret.)
3. from	One thing or person is different **from** another. (Never say **different to** or **different than.**)
4. in	This shows position in **one** place. (The king was **in** his counting-house.)
into	Shows movement from one place to another. (The boy fell from the tree **into** the river.)
5. past	This is a preposition and is always used with a verb. (The soldiers marched **past** the saluting base.)

Note: **Passed** is **not** a preposition but the **past tense** of the verb **pass.** (Mother **passed** the cake to Susan.)

EXERCISE 82

Pick out the **preposition** in each of these sentences.

1. There were four eggs in the blackbird's nest.
2. The deserter stared insolently at the officer.
3. Louis Blériot was the first man to fly across the English Channel.
4. The garage is situated behind the house.
5. Gerald and Dennis strolled through the wood.
6. Thousands of homes were bombed during the war.
7. The little terrier was under the table, fast asleep.
8. The defeated army fled from the battlefield.
9. The burglar climbed over the fence.
10. Raymond went to school very early this morning.

EXERCISE 83

Make up sentences using one of these **prepositions** in each.

1. about	6. before	11. down	16. behind
2. near	7. except	12. around	17. beyond
3. by	8. across	13. under	18. after
4. through	9. off	14. without	19. until
5. from	10. besides	15. below	20. during

Prepositions

Complete these sentences by using the correct **preposition** in each.

1. A stream of traffic stretched —— the road for two kilometres.
2. He vaulted nimbly —— the garden gate.
3. The cake was shared —— Mavis and Audrey.
4. A sword hung —— the head of Damocles.
5. Several visitors went —— the battleships during Navy Week.
6. The cake was divided —— the twelve boys in the class.
7. Mother Hubbard found nothing —— the cupboard.
8. The swimmer dived from the jetty —— the harbour.
9. The sailor swarmed —— the rope like a monkey.
10. The headmaster was angry —— the two truants.
11. The spectators were angry —— the referee's decisions.
12. The scout crept stealthily —— the sentry.
13. A red brick garage stood —— the large house.
14. Several boys —— Oliver arrived early.
15. We waited —— Peter to change his clothes.
16. A nurse waited —— mother during her illness.
17. Clive corresponds —— several pen friends abroad.
18. The workers protested —— the cut in wages.
19. The book is entirely different —— the last one I read.
20. Duncan is suffering —— rheumatism.

What are the missing **prepositions**?

1. according ——
2. disagree ——
3. shrink ——
4. inspired ——
5. similar ——

6. interfere ——
7. guilty ——
8. opposite ——
9. satisfied ——
10. victim ——

11. acquainted ——
12. comment ——
13. despair ——
14. rely ——
15. plunged ——

Capital Letters

We should learn when to use **capital letters,** for not only do they make reading easier but failure to use them betrays an ignorance of correct English. Below are several rules which show when **capital letters** are to be used.

LEARN THESE RULES

Capitals should be used:

1. For the first word of every sentence.

   Example: It was a glorious day yesterday.

2. For all surnames and Christian names.

   Examples: Hilda; Jane; Cecil; Smith; Thomson; Jones

3. For a person's initials.

   Examples: G. K. Chesterton; R.L.S. for Robert Louis Stevenson

4. To begin geographical names: towns, countries, rivers, lakes, mountains, etc.

   Examples: Bolton; France; Thames; Windermere; Snowdon

5. For the names of streets, roads, buildings, etc.

   Examples: High Street; Station Road; Eton College

6. For the titles of books, plays, newspapers, poems, songs, etc.

   Examples: Treasure Island; The Tempest; The Times; The Daffodils; Cherry Ripe

7. When writing the names of ships.

   Examples: H.M.S. Victory; Hispaniola; Golden Hind

8. For the names of the days of the week, the months of the year, and for special holidays.

   Examples: Wednesday; October; Easter

9. For the words **I** and **O,** which must never be in small letters.

10. For the first word of direct speech.

    Example: Mother said, "Close the door, please."

Capital Letters

11. For titles used before Proper Names.

> *Examples:* Prince Charles; Lord Nelson; Sir Francis Drake

12. For the names of God and Jesus Christ, as well as for pronouns relating to Them.

> *Examples:* The Saviour; The Messiah; He is our strength; Hallowed be Thy name

13. To begin every line of poetry

> *Example:* Day after day, day after day,
> We stuck, nor breath nor motion;
> As idle as a painted ship
> Upon a painted ocean.

EXERCISE 86

Rewrite these sentences, using **capital letters** where necessary.

1. alan invited michael to his birthday party.

2. france was liberated by british and american forces.

3. mount everest is the highest mountain in the world.

4. yesterday i told mother that i would be home early today.

5. at the school concert william recited the inchcape rock.

6. suddenly barry asked, "has anybody seen my bat?"

7. every easter janice spends a holiday at eastbourne.

8. the school party visited buckingham palace and westminster abbey.

9. christmas commemorates the birth of jesus christ.

10.   up the airy mountain,
                down the rushy glen;
            we daren't go a-hunting
                for fear of little men.

11. grandpa was sitting in his armchair reading the daily globe.

12. i have only just finished reading robinson crusoe.

72

EXERCISE 87

Write the answers to these questions, remembering that each must begin with a **capital letter.**

1. What is your full name?
2. What is the name of the street, road, avenue, etc. in which you live?
3. In what village, town or city do you live?
4. What is the name of the county in which it is situated?
5. What are the Christian names of your father and mother?
6. Who is the television personality you like best?
7. What is the title of your favourite book?
8. In which foreign country would you like to spend a holiday?
9. What was the name of Lord Nelson's flagship?
10. Which month of the year has most letters in its name?

EXERCISE 88

Write the words in this list which require a **capital letter.**

1. mountain
2. norway
3. measles
4. birmingham
5. alfred
6. stonehenge
7. atlantic
8. spaniard
9. city
10. ocean
11. language
12. month
13. nation
14. aladdin
15. dutch
16. country
17. sussex
18. pantomime
19. october
20. calendar

Agreement of Subject and Verb

The **subject** of a sentence must always agree with its **verb** in number. If the **subject is singular** then the **verb** must be **singular.** Similarly, a **plural subject** takes a **plural verb.**

First, find the subject.

Then find out whether it is singular or plural.

Example: The **boy goes** to bed early.

Boy, which is the subject of this sentence, is singular, so we must use a singular verb.

Example: The **boys go** to bed early.

Here, we have a plural subject, **boys,** and so a plural verb must be used.

Note: The commonest way of forming the plurals of nouns is by adding **-s** or **-es.**

Examples: girl — girl**s**; box — box**es**; brush — brush**es**

Most verbs form their singular number by adding **-s** or **-es**

Examples: say — say**s**; push — push**es**; do — do**es**

Now read these sentences:

(a) The price of pears —— too high. (**is, are**)

What is too high? The **price.**

As this is a singular noun we require a singular verb.

So we say: The price of pears **is** too high.

(b) The prices in that shop —— ridiculous. (**is, are**)

The subject is **prices,** not shop, and as this is plural we must use a plural verb.

The prices in that shop **are** ridiculous.

Collective Nouns

When a subject is a collective noun we must find out whether it is regarded as a unit or as several things.

Agreement of Subject and Verb

(a) The class —— warned not to throw stones. (**was, were**)

Here, the class is considered as a **unit,** so a singular verb must be used.

The class **was** warned not to throw stones.

(b) All the classes —— warned not to throw stones. (**was, were**)

Because classes is plural, a plural verb must be used.

All the classes **were** warned not to throw stones.

(c) The council —— to meet next Thursday. (**is, are**)

Because council refers to **one** body a singular verb is used.

The council **is** to meet next Thursday.

(d) The council —— unable to agree. (**is, are**)

Because the various members who make up the council are unable to agree we use a plural verb.

The council **are** unable to agree.

Sums and Quantities

Words denoting sums of money or quantities such as lengths, weights, etc. are considered as **units,** and take **singular** verbs.

Example: Twenty pence **was** all I had. (not **were**)

Six months **is** a long time to wait. (not **are**)

Note: Some nouns which appear to be plural because they end with -s are really singular.

Examples: Measles **is** an infectious disease.

The news **was** better last night.

Subjects with Two Nouns

When the subject consists of two (or more) nouns joined by **and** a plural verb is used.

Example: Health and happiness **are** priceless.

But if the two nouns are considered as **one** thing then the **singular** verb is used.

Example: Bread and butter **is** eaten at most meals.

Agreement of Subject and Verb

OR and NOR

If the subjects consists of two nouns joined by **or** or **nor** the singular verb is required.

Examples: Either the boy **or** his sister **is** telling lies.

Neither Amy **nor** Jo **was** at the party last night.

EXERCISE 89

Choose the right verb to complete these sentences.

1. The builder —— his work very thoroughly. (**do, does**)
2. Mumps —— a very painful ailment. (**is, are**)
3. The boy —— to school early every day. (**come, comes**)
4. Our dog —— bones. (**like, likes**)
5. The boys —— to school early every day. (**come, comes**)
6. All dogs —— bones. (**like, likes**)
7. The box of blocks —— dropped. (**was, were**)
8. —— the sky look beautiful today? (**Don't, Doesn't**)
9. The children always —— their books away. (**put, puts**)
10. Fish and chips —— a popular meal. (**is, are**)
11. Fish and meat —— two nourishing foods. (**is, are**)
12. Either William or Sally —— taken my pencil. (**has, have**)
13. One of the sailors —— killed in the accident. (**was, were**)
14. Fifty pence —— quite enough pocket-money for you. (**is, are**)
15. The cost of these houses —— me. (**shock, shocks**)
16. Mathematics —— my father's favourite subject. (**was, were**)
17. Neither of the full-backs in the school team —— in form yesterday. (**was, were**)
18. The school team —— top of the league last year. (**was, were**)
19. The school team —— to receive their medals next week. (**is, are**)
20. The number of motor-cars —— increasing. (**is, are**)

Agreement of Subject and Verb

Pronouns and Verbs

Most mistakes in Subject and Verb Agreement are made when the subject is a **pronoun.** Ungrammatical sentences like these are to be heard every day:

(a) You **was** late for the concert last night. (You **were** . . .)

(b) He **don't** come to the Boys' Club now. (He **doesn't** . . .)

(c) They **ain't** real pearls. (They **aren't** . . .)

(d) It **were** a cold and frosty night. (It **was** . . .)

This table will show you which number of the verb is used with certain pronouns.

He — She — It	I	We — You — They
is	am	are
was	was	were
does	do	do
has	have	have

These rules also apply when **not** is combined with these verbs:

isn't   aren't   wasn't   weren't   doesn't

don't   hasn't   haven't

Note: There is no such word as **ain't.**

Never say, "I **ain't** afraid of him."

Say, "I am not afraid of him."

"I'm not afraid of him."

EXERCISE 90

Complete these sentences by using the correct **verb.**

1. It —— look a very promising day. (**doesn't; don't**)
2. Perhaps she —— heard the news by now. (**has; have**)
3. They —— frightened out of their wits. (**was; were**)

Agreement of Subject and Verb

4. —— the referee know the rules? (**Doesn't; Don't**)
5. He —— slept a wink all night. (**hasn't; haven't**)
6. They —— drawings on the wallboards. (**does; do**)
7. —— you late for school this morning? (**Was; Were**)
8. It —— very warm at the seaside yesterday. (**was; were**)
9. He asked me if you —— my friend. (**was; were**)
10. He —— given his ball to Paul. (**has; have**)
11. I —— exercise every day. (**take; takes**)
12. You —— out early this morning. (**was; were**)
13. It —— rained for a week. (**hasn't; haven't**)
14. They —— the books I asked for. (**wasn't; weren't**)
15. —— she often go to church? (**Does; Do**)
16. He —— play for the school team now. (**doesn't; don't**)
17. I was sorry to hear you —— ill. (**was; were**)
18. We —— dead tired after our long walk. (**was; were**)
19. They —— flowers to be proud of. (**was; were**)
20. I —— to a football match every Saturday. (**goes; go**)

Here is a list of words which always take a **singular** verb.

each	**every**	**one**	**not one**
nobody	**no one**	**someone**	**somebody**
anyone	**anybody**	**everyone**	**everybody**

EXERCISE 91

Complete these sentences, using the **singular** or **plural** form of the **verb,** as required.

1. Every orange —— wrapped in silver paper. (**was; were**)
2. One of the players —— been hurt. (**has; have**)
3. Each member —— the right to vote. (**has; have**)
4. It looks as though everybody —— gone home. (**has; have**)
5. Every member —— the right to vote. (**has; have**)

Agreement of Subject and Verb

6. Each of the oranges —— wrapped in silver paper. (**was; were**)
7. Not one of the eggs —— been hatched. (**has; have**)
8. I hope that everyone —— enjoyed the party. (**has; have**)
9. All the oranges —— wrapped in silver paper. (**was; were**)
10. I hope somebody in our class —— the prize. (**get; gets**)
11. All members —— the right to vote. (**has; have**)
12. One of you two boys —— telling lies. (**is; are**)
13. In our class no one —— any interest in stamp-collecting. (**take; takes**)
14. —— every child had enough to eat? (**Has; Have**)
15. Each of the forwards —— playing magnificently. (**was; were**)
16. None of our dogs —— awarded a prize. (**was; were**)
17. Every one of the babies —— vaccinated. (**was; were**)
18. Somebody —— broken my new fountain pen. (**has; have**)
19. —— anyone know our teacher's address? (**Do; Does**)
20. One of our girls —— lost her purse. (**has; have**)

Sentences

We convey our thoughts to other people in the form of sentences, both when we speak and when we write, so it is very important that we should be able to compose good sentences.

We can say that:

> A SENTENCE is a group of words which expresses a complete thought; in other words, it makes sense.

For example, this group of words does not make sense:

if you cannot come

But if we place the words 'write and let me know' **either before or after it** we have a complete sentence. We know exactly what is meant.

Before: Write and let me know **if you cannot come.**

After: **If you cannot come** write and let me know.

EXERCISE 92

Here are ten groups of words; say which of them form complete sentences and which do not by writing YES or NO after the number in each case.

Examples: With a light heart. *Answer:* No

Martin ate all his lunch. *Answer:* Yes

1. One evening in May
2. The children went to the circus.
3. Into the deep end of the swimming bath
4. In the very heart of Africa
5. The seat on an elephant's back is called a howdah.
6. Before the sun had risen above the horizon
7. Guy Fawkes was put to death for his part in the Gunpowder Plot.
8. John Ridd tumbled from the back of the highwayman's horse.
9. Would you like to come with me?
10. From early in the morning till late in the evening

To make sense the words in a sentence must be arranged in a certain order. Consider these words:

The the chased boy dog.

As they stand they have no meaning at all, but by arranging them in a different order we can make the sentence:

The boy chased the dog.

But if we arrange them in another order we can make a sentence which conveys the opposite meaning:

The dog chased the boy.

EXERCISE 93

Below you will find ten groups of words, each of which will make a complete sentence when arranged in proper order. Write these sentences correctly.

Remember that every sentence begins with a capital letter and ends with a full stop, a question mark or an exclamation mark.

1. Sir built Wren Cathedral was by St. Christopher Paul's
2. fine for manufacture is the noted cutlery of Sheffield
3. the country set up William in this Caxton printing press first
4. but is not the fish a mammal a whale
5. the young pouch in a kangaroo carries its
6. France for food snails are used in
7. rough tree a very trunk has elm the
8. all the leaves of decaying earthworm will eat kinds
9. canoes called Eskimos go frail in skin kayaks fishing
10. the talons with its eagle seizes its strong prey

EXERCISE 94

Now write ten sentences of your own, using the three words given in each case. The example shows you what is required.

Sentences

Example: **farmer — tractor — fields**

Answer: The modern **farmer** uses a **tractor** to plough his **fields.**

1. boy — football — window
2. gorilla — cage — keeper
3. monkeys — coconuts — hunters
4. soldier — officer — saluted
5. mother — frock — material
6. cat — table — milk
7. children — storm — barn
8. cowboy — dust — road
9. highwayman — coach — passengers
10. fox — farmyard — ducks

EXERCISE 95

Make sentences of your own by copying the words below and writing a few suitable words after them.

1. On the way to school we ....
2. The hunter raised his rifle and ....
3. With a deep growl the bulldog ....
4. The sailor told the children that ....
5. In spring the farmer is busy ....
6. After the party the children ....
7. When Jeremy lost his ball ....
8. One day last summer holidays ....
9. At the entrance to the football ground ....
10. As he had no money left ....

EXERCISE 96

Write ten sentences of your own about ten different animals found either in a zoo or on a farm.

Example: The cow is a very useful animal, for it provides us with milk, from which butter and cheese are made.

Sentences

EXERCISE 97

Write a few words of your own before each group of words in this exercise so as to form a complete sentence in each case.

1. .... rescued the child from the burning house.
2. .... galloped away down the road.
3. .... directed us to the Art Gallery.
4. .... is mined in South Wales.
5. .... held up his hand and stopped the traffic.
6. .... was strewn with fallen leaves.
7. .... laughed until their sides ached.
8. .... was too stiff to move.
9. .... was arrested by two policemen.
10. .... are imported into Britain from Australia.

EXERCISE 98

Both columns below contain parts of sentences. Write each part from Column A, then choose the part in Column B which matches it.

Column A	Column B
1. Simon was feeling tired	A. cruised leisurely round the sunlit bay.
2. Foxes leave on their trail	B. are made of ivory.
3. Of the Seven Wonders of the Ancient World	C. James learnt how to surf-ride.
4. The powerful racing-car	D. a strong scent from glands in their feet.
5. Because of ill-health	E. only the Pyramids remain.
6. The life of Egypt	F. so he went to bed.
7. The tusks of the elephant	G. lived in a log cabin when he was a boy.
8. The little pleasure boat	H. sped round the track at a record speed.
9. Whilst visiting Hawaii in the Pacific	I. Robert Louis Stevenson travelled a great deal.
10. Abraham Lincoln, sixteenth President of the U.S.A.,	J. has always been centred on the River Nile.

Speech

In writing conversation the actual words used by a speaker are always enclosed in inverted commas, or quotation marks as they are sometimes called. (" and ")

Example: **" I have just finished reading this book," said Martin.**

The **actual** words spoken by Martin were:

"I have just finished reading this book."

Notice the inverted commas (") **before** the **first** word spoken and those (") **after** the **last** word spoken.

The quotation marks " always come **after** a comma or other punctuation mark at the end of conversation, and **never before, or directly above.**

Wrong	**Wrong**	**Right**
...........book",	...........book".	...........book,"

EXERCISE 99

Insert quotation marks where necessary in these sentences. All are of the same type as the example, with the spoken words coming **first.**

1. Has morning come already? asked Nicholas, sitting up in bed.
2. Your dinner is ready, Ronald, said Mrs. Stevens.
3. What are you doing here? cried the Selfish Giant in a gruff voice, and the children ran away.
4. I can run faster than any boy in school, boasted Jack.
5. As soon as Mr. Joyce comes I shall be going out, announced father.
6. What terribly rough weather we are having this week! exclaimed the caravanner.
7. Does Mrs. Phillips live here, please? inquired Gillian.
8. Oh, please let me go, pleaded Peter as the bully seized him by the ear.
9. Susan's apple is bigger than mine, grumbled Ann.
10. Here's Ralph. Let's hide behind this bush, whispered Donald.

Speech

Next, look at this sentence.

Jennifer said, "Look at this dear little puppy."

Here, the **unspoken words** come first.

Notice that **the first word spoken begins with a capital letter.**

The sentences below are all of this type.

EXERCISE 100

Insert the necessary **quotation marks** in these sentences.

1. Richard heard loud singing and laughter, then someone said, tending your horse, sir?

2. Placing the megaphone to his mouth the mate bellowed, ship ahoy!

3. In a loud voice the Wolf said angrily, what do you mean by making the water in the stream muddy?

4. In half a minute the window was opened again, and the same voice called out to Pinocchio, stand under the window and hold up your cap.

5. Alice hastily put down the bottle, saying to herself, that's quite enough—I hope I shan't grow any more.

6. Michael, who knew the way, asked, does the King live here?

7. Just then the master happened to look up, and exclaimed, angrily, John Ward, who blacked your face?

8. The Doctor only asked one question, you know that you are not allowed to fish from the bank opposite the school, Brown?

9. With a polite little bow the chicken said cheerfully, a thousand thanks Mr. Pinocchio for having spared me the trouble of breaking the shell.

10. Going up to her mother Janet whispered, please Mummy, may I have five pence to buy some chocolate?

85

Speech

In the third type of conversation the **unspoken words** come between the spoken words. This is sometimes called a broken quotation.

Example:

"Come near the fire," said Mrs. Dale, "and warm your hands."

Notice that **two pairs of quotation marks are used.**

The sentences which follow are all of this type.

EXERCISE 101

Insert the necessary **quotation marks** in these sentences.

1. There, said the schoolmaster, as they stepped in together, this
   is our shop, Nickleby.

2. That's the judge, said Alice to herself, because of his great wig.

3. My address, said Mr. Micawber, is Windsor Terrace, City Road.

4. Hallo! growled Scrooge, what do you mean by coming here at
   this time of day?

5. Come along, shouted Peter to Heidi, we have a long way to
   go yet.

6. Ride her! I cried with the bravest scorn. There never was a
   horse upon Exmoor foaled I could not tackle in half an hour.

7. O, Father, sobbed Maggie, I ran away because I was so unhappy.

8. Go and poke the fire, Martin Rattler, said the schoolmaster,
   and put on a bit of coal.

9. Perhaps it has been buried for ten years, whispered Mistress
   Mary. Perhaps it is the key to the garden.

10. Call off thy dogs, warned Little John, or they are likely to be
    hurt.

Speech

Change these sentences to **Indirect Speech.**

Example: "Switch on the light, John," said his mother. (*Direct*)
John's mother told him to switch on the light. (*Indirect*)

1. "Have you posted the letters, Kenneth?" asked Mr. Watkins.
2. "It is raining cats and dogs," remarked Uncle James.
3. "School will reopen on September 3rd," announced the headmaster.
4. "Janet," said her mother, "will you help to make the beds?"
5. "This medicine will soon put you right, Stephen," said Dr. Anderson.
6. "Is your mother at home, Maisie?" asked Mrs. Duncan.
7. "These eggs are not fresh," complained Mrs. Higgins to the grocer.
8. "Mind you don't burn your fingers with the fireworks, Bernard," warned his father.
9. "Has anyone seen my daily paper?" inquired Mr. Trent.
10. "Help!" shouted the drowning man.

Change these sentences to **Direct Speech.**

Example: Pauline told David to sit still. (*Indirect*)
"Sit still, David," said Pauline. (*Direct*)

1. Rodney's teacher asked him if he had read Oliver Twist.
2. Grandpa complained that the cushion was too hard.
3. Wilson said that he felt tired and would go to bed.
4. The seaman reported that the cabins were flooded.
5. Mrs. Hollins remarked that she would be ninety next birthday.
6. Dennis told Roger that he had just found a pound note.
7. Father exclaimed that it was ridiculous to expect a child to do three hours' homework.
8. The vicar announced that the Harvest Thanksgiving Service would be held on September 21st.
9. Ruth's teacher asked her why she was absent yesterday.
10. Raymond asked his mother if she would mend the hole in his pullover.

Alphabetical Order

The words in a dictionary are arranged in alphabetical order.

A B C D E F G H I J K L M N O P Q R S T U V W X Y Z

Words beginning with the letter **a** come first, but even these are arranged in a certain order which is determined by succeeding letters in the word.

Examples:

1st letter annual comes before centre because **a** comes before **c**.

2nd letter dark comes before desk because **a** comes before **e**.

3rd letter pedal comes before perch because **d** comes before **r**.

4th letter real comes before reap because **l** comes before **p**.

5th letter screen comes before screw because **e** comes before **w**.

EXERCISE 104

Arrange in alphabetical order.

1st letter

1. herald	arch	zebra	marble	jolly
2. plague	dainty	trough	youth	inkwell
3. chair	wheel	nerve	rake	glacier

2nd letter

4. measles	music	march	monk	middle
5. dormouse	drag	ditch	duke	defend
6. heart	halt	hurry	horse	hinder

3rd letter

7. drop	drudge	drill	drain	dress
8. flush	flash	flour	flesh	flint
9. spend	sponge	spur	spill	space

4th letter

10. shrink	shrapnel	shrug	shred	shroud
11. brook	brother	brown	broad	broke
12. lane	lantern	lance	land	language

5th letter

13. strict	string	stripe	stride	strike
14. strange	straw	straggle	strap	straight
15. porter	portrait	portion	portable	portmanteau

Contractions

When we speak, and often when we write, we might find it necessary to combine two words to form one word.

Example: **God's** in His heaven—
All's right with the world.

In full this would be:

God is in His heaven—
All is right with the world.

But it does not sound so well that way, does it? It lacks rhythm; the beauty of the lines is spoilt by the jerkiness with which they are spoken.

Instead of writing **all is** Robert Browning, the poet, wrote **all's.** The letter **i** was dropped from the word **is,** and the apostrophe (') was used to show this.

The word **contract** means **to become smaller,** so these shortened forms are called **contractions.**

Here is a list of **contractions** in common use, classified according to their combining words.

NOT	isn't	wasn't	doesn't	hasn't	can't
	won't	mustn't	mightn't	aren't	weren't
	don't	haven't	shan't	didn't	wouldn't
	shouldn't	needn't			
IS	he's	she's	it's	there's	who's
	where's	what's	that's	how's	
HAS	(The same as for **IS**).				
ARE	we're	you're	they're		
HAVE	I've	you've	we've	they've	where've
WILL	I'll	you'll	he'll	she'll	we'll
	they'll	there'll	it'll		
WOULD	I'd	you'd	he'd	she'd	we'd
	they'd	there'd	who'd		
AM	I'm				

Contractions

Study these lines from well-known poems, then write the contractions they contain in a column and opposite each write its full form.

Example: "Now **don't** go till I come," he said.
(**don't**—do not)

1. It's April, and blossom time, and white is the may.
   (*The West Wind*—John Masefield)

2. "There's a porpoise close behind us, and he's treading on my tail."
   (*The Lobster Quadrille*—Lewis Carroll)

3. "I'll go to my tower on the Rhine," replied he.
   (*Bishop Hatto*—Robert Southey)

4. "Here's a treasure I've found; what a feast it will be."
   (*The Mouse and the Cake*—Eliza Cook)

5. "But I'd give my soul for the smell o' the pitch,"
   Says he, "in Plymouth Sound."
   (*The Admiral's Ghost*—Alfred Noyes)

6. Said Francis then, "Faith, gentlemen, we're better here than there."
   (*The Glove and the Lions*—Leigh Hunt)

7. "I'm an owl; you're another. Sir Critic, good-day!"
   (*The Owl-Critic*—James T. Fields)

8. "And what's dead can't come to life, I think."
   (*The Pied Piper of Hamelin*—Robert Browning)

9. "The spider up there defied despair;
   He conquered, and why shouldn't I?"
   (*Try Again*—Eliza Cook)

10. We'll honour yet the school we knew.
    (*The Best School of All*—Henry Newbolt)

Contractions

Each of the following sentences contains two words from which a **contraction** can be formed. Write, in a column, the two words in each case, and opposite them write their shortened form.

Example: He **does not** live in this street now.

(**does not**—doesn't)

1. You are very much taller than Mary.
2. We have had a very mild winter this year.
3. You had better take a taxi to the station.
4. The farmer would not believe the poacher's story.
5. Jennifer is not taking part in the play.
6. Flies do not bother us in the winter.
7. Sally has not been absent once this year.
8. "You shall not have my orange," growled Bill.
9. "You must not be late for school," warned the teacher.
10. The swallow does not spend the winter in this country.
11. "Who has been sitting in my chair?" squeaked Baby Bear.
12. There will be buns for tea today.
13. "Who would like to come to the sports?" asked Father.
14. "I have not had my chocolate," grumbled Paul.
15. She will be coming round the mountain.
16. The crow could not reach the water in the pitcher.
17. There were not any apples left on the tree.
18. Peter has sprained his ankle and will not be able to play.
19. "I am sure I locked the front door," said Mother.
20. The girls are not going to play rounders.

Points to Remember

1. Contractions are used chiefly in conversation and in friendly letters. When writing a composition it is better to write the words in full.

2. When using contractions always remember to use the correct number of the verb. For example, you should not say:

"He **don't** like playing rugby."

Say, "He **doesn't** like playing rugby."

Contractions

3. There is no such contraction as **ain't,** although it is commonly used in speech in certain parts of the country.

Wrong: I **ain't** going to do it.   We **ain't** worrying.

Right: **I'm not** going to do it.   We **aren't** worrying.

4. Learn to distinguish between **whose** and **who's.**

Examples: **Whose** book is this? (*Possession*)

Who's coming to the match? (*Who is*)

5. Learn the difference between **its** and **it's.**

Examples: The dog hurt **its** paw. (*Possession*)

I think **it's** going to rain. (*it is*)

EXERCISE 107

Complete each sentence by using the correct word chosen from those in brackets.

1. A dog wags —— tail when —— pleased. (**its; it's**)

2. The teacher asked —— fountain pen it was. (**who's; whose**)

3. I —— got your cricket ball. (**haven't; ain't**)

4. Tony thinks —— a lovely little puppy. (**its; it's**)

5. That's the boy –—— father was injured. (**who's; whose**)

6. I hope you —— wet. (**ain't; aren't**)

7. We want to know —— to pay for the outing. (**who's; whose**)

8. Robert —— like swimming. (**doesn't; don't**)

9. —— to say —— fault it is? (**who's; whose**)

10. They —— come to our house very often now. (**doesn't; don't**)

Opposites

absent	present	empty	full
accept	refuse	enemy	friend
admit	deny	entrance	exit
advance	retreat	exterior	interior
ancient	modern	external	internal
arrival	departure	failure	success
artificial	genuine	false	true
assemble	disperse	famine	glut
attack	defence	folly	wisdom
backwards	forwards	foolish	wise
beautiful	ugly	forbid	permit
bent	straight	found	lost
better	worse	fresh	stale
bitter	sweet	future	past
bless	curse	generous	selfish
blunt	sharp	guilty	innocent
bold	timid	hatred	love
bravery	cowardice	heavy	light
bright	dull	help	hinder
broad	narrow	hollow	solid
build	demolish	humble	proud
captivity	freedom	hurry	loiter
capture	release	ignorance	knowledge
cautious	reckless	inferior	superior
celebrated	unknown	junior	senior
cheap	expensive	majority	minority
coarse	fine	masculine	feminine
compulsory	voluntary	maximum	minimum
conceal	reveal	miser	spendthrift
conceited	modest	noisy	quiet
contract	expand	peace	war
coward	hero	often	seldom
create	destroy	opaque	transparent
danger	safety	permanent	temporary
deep	shallow	plentiful	scarce
defeat	victory	plural	singular
difficult	easy	poverty	wealth
divide	multiply	punishment	reward
drunk	sober	rough	smooth
dwarf	giant		

Opposites

A word which is opposite in meaning to
another word is called an ANTONYM.

The opposites of words can often be formed by using a **prefix**,
that is a syllable written **before** it, such as **un, dis, in, ir, il, im,** etc.

Using the prefix -un

unarmed	uncertain	unequal	unfriendly
unhealthy	undress	uncommon	unhappy
unpopular	unsuitable	unwelcome	ungrateful
untrue	unwilling	unskilled	unreasonable
unwise	unreliable	unconscious	unsteady

EXERCISE 108

Complete these sentences by using the **antonyms** beginning
with **-un.**

1. When you take off your clothes you **un**——.
2. An **un**—— person is miserable.
3. An **un**—— person gives no thanks for the favours he receives.
4. An **un**—— soldier carries no weapons.
5. If you are **un**—— about something you are doubtful about it.
6. An **un**—— person often has to consult a doctor.
7. When a person has been knocked **un**—— he does not know
   what is going on around him.
8. A rumour which is false is **un**——.
9. An **un**—— person is one who is disliked.
10. An **un**—— workman is one who is untrained.

Using the prefix -in

incapable	insane	invisible	ingratitude
incomplete	indirect	inaudible	inexpensive
incorrect	incurable	inattentive	independent
insincere	injustice	inefficient	inequality
indistinct	indecent	inoffensive	insufficient

94

EXERCISE 109

Complete these sentences by using **antonyms** beginning with **in-**.

1. An **in**—— article does not cost very much.
2. An **in**—— route is a roundabout way.
3. An **in**—— is an act which lacks justice.
4. A sum which is **in**—— is wrong.
5. An **in**—— person is mad.
6. An object which is out of sight is **in**——.
7. A pupil who is not paying attention to a lesson is **in**——.
8. A jig-saw puzzle from which pieces are missing is **in**——.
9. An **in**—— person does not offend anybody.
10. An **in**—— disease is one which cannot be cured.

Using the prefix dis-

disappear	discomfort	disconnect	dissatisfied
disloyal	disbelieve	discourteous	disadvantage
dishonest	disarm	disorderly	discontented
disagree	disobedient	disallow	disarrange
dislike	discontinue	displeasure	disrespectful

EXERCISE 110

Use **antonyms** beginning with **dis-** to complete these sentences.

1. A servant who robs or cheats his master is **dis**——.
2. The word **dis**—— means to go out of sight.
3. A **dis**—— child does not do as he is told.
4. People who **dis**—— hold different points of view.
5. A **dis**—— person is lacking in courtesy.
6. To **dis**—— a person is to take his weapons from him.
7. A **dis**—— boy has no respect for others.
8. **Dis**—— people are not contented with their lot.
9. When you **dis**—— something you remove it from something to which it is connected.
10. When winds **dis**—— a girl's hair they disturb the arrangement of it.

Opposites

The opposites of many words ending with **-ful** are formed by substituting **-less** for **-ful**.

Examples:

hopeful	hopeless	powerful	powerless
painful	painless	doubtful	doubtless
careful	careless	shameful	shameless
harmful	harmless	helpful	helpless
cheerful	cheerless	restful	restless
pitiful	pitiless	thoughtful	thoughtless
useful	useless	thankful	thankless

EXERCISE 111

Insert an adjective ending with **-ful** or **-less** in each space in these sentences.

1. Toothache is a very —— ailment.

2. Many racing cars have —— engines.

3. The viper is a poisonous snake but the grass snake is quite ——.

4. A blunt knife is quite ——.

5. Children should be —— for good parents.

6. Hugh had six sums wrong due to —— working.

7. A blazing log fire helps to make a room ——.

8. A —— person can do nothing for himself.

9. Howard is ill and it is —— whether he will be in school today.

10. In the desert the travellers could find no shade from the —— rays of the sun.

11. Severe toothache caused Richard to have a —— night.

12. Only a very —— craftsman could make such a beautiful piece of furniture.

13. At Easter-time eggs are usually ——.

14. He was such a —— business man that he became a millionaire.

15. The people made —— by the floods were given food and shelter in the Town Hall.

Opposites

Using im-, il-, ir-, or non-.

immovable	illegal	nonsense
improbable	illegible	non-existent
imperfect	illiterate	non-intoxicating
impatient	irregular	non-essential
immortal	irresistible	improper
impossible	irresponsible	impolite
impure	irreverent	impenetrable

EXERCISE 112

Use one of the above words to fill the space in each of these sentences.

1. An **im**—— object **cannot be moved.**

2. Children who are often absent from school are **ir**—— in attendance.

3. A **non**—— beverage will not make one drunk.

4. When people do not talk sense they are talking **non**——.

5. Dirty water is **im**——.

6. An **il**—— àct is unlawful.

7. An **im**—— feat or task is one that cannot be done.

8. An **im**—— event is one which is not likely to happen.

9. We can do without **non**—— articles.

0. An **im**—— person is lacking in good manners.

1. The doctor's writing was **il**——.

2. The children were **im**—— at the delay.

3. **Il**—— people are those who **cannot read and** write.

4. The stockings were sold at reduced prices because they were **im**——.

5. The temptation to taste mother's cakes was **ir**——.

97

Opposites

Write the **opposites** of the following words.

1. enemy	6. divide	11. defeat	16. wisdom
2. generous	7. help	12. ignorance	17. broad
3. bold	8. wealth	13. conceal	18. dwarf
4. proud	9. attack	14. success	19. bent
5. heroic	10. love	15. transparent	20. assemble

Rewrite these sentences, substituting the **opposites** of the words in heavy type.

1. Uncle David **often** comes to our house.
2. The **minimum** salary is £1500 a year.
3. Vast crowds cheered the M.C.C. on their **arrival.**
4. The **interior** of the school is to be painted.
5. Mr. Green's job is a **temporary** one.
6. The church is quite an **ancient** building.
7. Both blades of this pocket-knife are very **sharp.**
8. The general ordered his troops to **advance.**
9. Mary's writing is much **better** than it used to be.
10. This sandpaper is too **fine.**

In each line below select the word which is **opposite** in meaning to the word in heavy type.

1. **contract**   expand; subtract; attract; decrease
2. **prohibit**   exhibit; protect; permit; forbid
3. **transparent**   coloured; apparent; brittle; opaque
4. **reckless**   stubborn; needless; cautious; careless
5. **economy**   gratitude; thrift; miserliness; extravagance
6. **sudden**   momentary; temporary; gradual; permanent
7. **voluntary**   compulsory; preparatory; satisfactory; necessary
8. **freedom**   festivity; humility; ability; captivity
9. **conceited**   anxious; modest; deceitful; proud
10. **inferior**   exterior; interior; junior; superior

Opposites

Write each pair of **opposite words** found in each line below.

1.	stage	comic	theatre	tragic	company
2.	admit	permit	deny	prove	prosecute
3.	massive	beautiful	artificial	expensive	genuine
4.	resemble	announce	pronounce	assemble	disperse
5.	extensive	barren	fertile	pasture	meadow
6.	create	dictate	destroy	surround	magnify
7.	resistance	assistance	instance	remittance	hindrance
8.	internal	eternal	external	inferior	infernal
9.	command	remand	demand	compare	obey
10.	priority	majority	security	minority	impurity

Complete each sentence by using the **opposite** of one of the words contained in it.

Example: He intends to work harder in the —— than he has in the **past.**

Answer: **future**

1. After the examination the boy felt more dead than ——.
2. We might as well do the weeding first as ——.
3. Henry had nine sums right and one ——.
4. One boy knew the answer to every ——.
5. Wise people ·save money; —— people spend all they earn.
6. Eggs are plentiful in spring, but —— in winter.
7. Seeing that the children were in danger, the policeman removed them to a place of ——.
8. The river was deep in some parts but quite —— in others.
9. The father is a miser, but the son is a ——.
10. The man said he was innocent, but the police proved him ——.

For each word below write an **antonym** of **five** letters.

1. clean	6. lost	11. noisy	16. back
2. bold	7. asleep	12. true	17. dwarf
3. hollow	8. full	13. expensive	18. humble
4. late	9. bless	14. light	19. war
5. long	10. loiter	15. narrow	20. friend

Synonyms

Harder Word	Easier Word	Harder Word	Easier Word
abandon	leave	comprehend	understand
abbreviate	shorten	conceal	hide
abode	dwelling	conclusion	end
abrupt	sudden	conversation	talk
abundant	plentiful	countenance	face
accommodation	room	courageous	brave
accurate	correct	courteous	polite
adversity	misfortune	deceive	cheat
aggressive	quarrelsome	deficiency	shortage
altitude	height	demonstrate	show
amiable	friendly	denounce	condemn
ample	plentiful	deride	mock
animosity	hatred	desert	forsake
annual	yearly	despise	scorn
anonymous	nameless	detest	hate
anticipate	expect	diminish	lessen
apparel	clothes	diminutive	small
apparition	ghost	disperse	scatter
arrogant	haughty	drowsy	sleepy
assembly	gathering	dubious	doubtful
assistance	help	edible	eatable
astonishment	surprise	elude	escape
attired	dressed	eminent	famous
audacity	impudence	encircle	surround
austere	severe	endeavour	attempt
avaricious	greedy	energetic	active
beverages	drinks	enormous	huge
brief	short	excavate	dig
catastrophe	disaster	exhibit	show
cautious	careful	extravagance	waste
cease	stop	fatigue	weariness
celebrated	famous	ferocious	fierce
centre	middle	frigid	cold
chivalrous	gallant	generous	kind
circular	round	gorgeous	splendid
colossal	huge	gleaming	shining
commence	begin	gratitude	thankfulness
compel	force	grave	serious

Synonyms

Harder Word	Easier Word
gruesome	horrible
indolent	lazy
industrious	busy
infuriated	angry
inquire	ask
insane	mad
insolent	cheeky
intention	purpose
interior	inside
intoxicated	drunk
invaluable	priceless
invincible	unbeatable
jovial	jolly
lofty	high
loathe	hate
lubricate	oil
mammoth	huge
margin	edge
mariner	sailor
matrimony	marriage
maximum	most
mechanism	machinery
melancholy	sad
minimum	least
moist	damp
motionless	still
mute	dumb
necessity	need
obstinate	stubborn
odour	smell
omen	sign
option	choice
pandemonium	uproar
pathetic	pitiful
peculiar	odd
penetrate	pierce
perceive	see
persuade	coax

Harder Word	Easier Word
peruse	read
portion	part
procure	obtain
prohibit	forbid
prominent	outstanding
prompt	quick
puny	weak
purloin	steal
putrid	rotten
rare	scarce
reckless	rash
recollect	remember
regret	sorrow
reluctant	unwilling
reveal	show
robust	strong
ruddy	red
scanty	scarce
sever	separate
significance	importance
slender	slim
solitude	loneliness
spectre	ghost
squander	waste
stationary	still
sufficient	enough
summit	top
tempestuous	stormy
tranquil	calm
unite	join
vacant	empty
valiant	brave
vanquish	conquer
velocity	speed
wealthy	rich
wrath	anger
wretched	miserable
youthful	young

Synonyms

Rewrite these sentences, using a simpler word in place of each word in heavy type.

1. Herrings were **abundant** in the North Sea.
2. The hunter did not **perceive** the tiger which was lying in wait for him.
3. The injured boy's face was a **pathetic** sight.
4. John's face wore a **melancholy** expression.
5. We took four hours to reach the **summit** of the mountain.
6. A heavy meal tends to make one **drowsy.**
7. Every Saturday Dennis **lubricates** his bicycle.
8. The bungalow has been **vacant** for some time.
9. The farmer's son had grown into a **robust** lad.
10. Mother did her best to **procure** a school scarf for Harold.

In each line below select the word which has a **similar** meaning to the word in heavy type.

1. **adversity:**	enemy	misfortune	building	joy
2. **valiant:**	boastful	sorrowful	brave	disgraceful
3. **eminent:**	clever	ambitious	cunning	famous
4. **jovial:**	jolly	melancholy	stubborn	willing
5. **dubious:**	certain	doubtful	vigorous	feeble
6. **deficiency:**	skill	exercise	shortage	enough
7. **audacity:**	courage	timidity	politeness	impudence
8. **fatigue:**	weariness	stoutness	deceit	duty
9. **indolent:**	bankrupt	lazy	cheeky	silent
10. **prohibit:**	display	permit	forbid	advertise

In place of each word below write a **synonym** beginning with the letter **S.**

1. begin	6. odour	11. mariner	16. powerful
2. disperse	7. astonishment	12. cosy	17. quiet
3. cunning	8. reveal	13. scanty	18. regret
4. grasp	9. motionless	14. omen	19. abrupt
5. grave	10. cease	15. frighten	20. choose

Synonyms

In each line below there are **two words** which are **similar** in meaning. Write these words.

1. midday   dawn   morning   evening   sunrise
2. hideous   detestable splendid   gorgeous   ordinary
3. expand   examine   decrease   dwindle   improve
4. foretell   foremost   lowest   leading   honest
5. faithful   fortunate   lucky   successful   industrious
6. fertility   enmity   happiness   hostility   friendship
7. edge   slope   summit   brink   precipice
8. loiter   hasten   linger   postpone   arrange
9. invisible   inevitable invincible divisible   unconquerable
10. loathe   explore   detest   deplore   implore

In place of each word in heavy type write a word of **five** letters which has a **similar** meaning.

1. The largest flower-bed is **circular** in shape.
2. The captain refused to **abandon** his ship.
3. The **minimum** quantity supplied is one kilogram.
4. The men **commenced** work at 9 a.m.
5. Arthur was commended for his **courageous** conduct.
6. We should not **squander** our money.
7. Two boys **attempted** to lift the heavy bag.
8. The sergeant gave vent to his **wrath.**
9. With milk and cordials many a delicious **beverage** can be made.
10. Scrooge saw the **apparition** coming towards him.

For each word below give a word of **five** letters which has a **similar** meaning.

1. deceive   6. commence   11. coarse   16. extravagance
2. brief   7. steed   12. mistake   17. diminutive
3. odour   8. infuriated 13. spectre   18. despise
4. wrath   9. courageous 14. compel   19. stationary
5. purloin   10. intoxicated 15. velocity 20. youthful

Synonyms

Four of the five words in each row below are **similar** in meaning; the other is different. Write the words which have a **different** meaning.

1.	small	weak	little	tiny	miniature
2.	hurricane	typhoon	torpedo	tornado	cyclone
3.	tall	slight	slim	slender	thin
4.	obstruct	hamper	hinder	assist	impede
5.	still	quiet	silent	noiseless	rowdy
6.	strong	fat	stout	portly	plump
7.	part	piece	mass	portion	fragment
8.	journey	tour	expedition	excursion	arrangement
9.	revolution	rebellion	revolt	riot	resurrection
10.	ridicule	praise	scorn	mock	taunt

Match the words in column A with those of **similar** meaning in column B. Write the numbers and letters only.

Example: **1. E.**

Column A	Column B
1. chivalrous	A. rotten
2. aggressive	B. horrible
3. tranquil	C. cold
4. reluctant	D. huge
5. gruesome	E. gallant
6. invincible	F. quarrelsome
7. amiable	G. calm
8. putrid	H. unwilling
9. frigid	I. unbeatable
10. colossal	J. friendly

EXERCISE 127

Rewrite these sentences using **one word** in place of the words in heavy type.

1. I must return home **without delay.**

2. Graham **made up his mind** to do better work next term.

3. I will see you when you **come back again.**

4. Sylvia handed the book to the **man in charge of the library.**

5. You can throw that ball-pen away; it is **of no use.**

6. **All of a sudden** the horse bolted and leaped over a low hedge.

7. The poor woman was **not in her right mind.**

8. Brian worked all the sums **without making a single mistake.**

9. When he reached the enclosure the jockey **got down from his horse.**

EXERCISE 128

Give **one word** which means the same as those in heavy type in each of the following sentences.

1. Ann **removed the wrappings from** her Christmas parcels.

2. I opened the windows to **let air into the** room.

3. The **woman in charge** of the hospital was decorated by the Queen.

4. In spring the days begin to **get longer.**

5. The sailor **saved the life of** the drowning boy.

6. We watched the flywheel **turn round and round** at high speed.

7. The star became smaller and smaller, then **went out of sight** completely.

8. A party of children from our school visited Belgium **not long ago.**

9. The pearl necklace is **not genuine.**

10. The **man who collects the refuse** complained that the dustbin was too heavy.

Homophones

air	heir		hair	hare
aisle	isle		hall	haul
allowed	aloud		heal	heel
bail	bale		hear	here
ball	bawl		heard	herd
bare	bear		higher	hire
beach	beech		him	hymn
bean	been		hoard	horde
beat	beet		hole	whole
berth	birth		hour	our
blew	blue		idle	idol
board	bored		key	quay
bough	bow		knead	need
boy	buoy		knew	new
brake	break		knight	night
buy	by / bye		knot	not
ceiling	sealing		knows	nose
cell	sell		lain	lane
cent	sent / scent		lead	led
cereal	serial		leak	leek
check	cheque		lessen	lesson
coarse	course		lightening	lightning
currant	current		loan	lone
dear	deer		made	maid
die	dye		mail	male
draft	draught		main	mane
faint	feint		mantel	mantle
fair	fare		mare	mayor
feat	feet		meat	meet
find	fined		medal	meddle
fir	fur		missed	mist
flea	flee		muscle	mussel
flew	flue		none	nun
flour	flower		oar	ore
fore	four		one	won
foul	fowl		pail	pale
gamble	gambol		pain	pane
gilt	guilt		pair	pear / pare
grate	great		pause	paws
groan	grown		peace	piece
			peal	peel

106

peer	pier	sight	site
place	plaice	soar	sore
plum	plumb	sole	soul
pore	pour	son	sun
practice	practise	stair	stare
pray	prey	stake	steak
principal	principle	stationary	stationery
profit	prophet	steal	steel
rain	reign / rein	stile	style
		tail	tale
raise	rays / raze	tear	tier
		their	there
rap	wrap	threw	through
read	reed	throne	thrown
read	red	thyme	time
right	write	tide	tied
ring	wring	told	tolled
road	rode / rowed	vain	vane / vein
role	roll	vale	veil
root	route	waist	waste
sail	sale	wait	weight
scene	seen	weak	week
sea	see	wood	would
seam	seem	yoke	yolk
sew	sow		

Homophones

Read this verse from Thomas Hood's poem *Faithless Sally Brown*. It tells us what happened to Young Ben, who was in love with Sally, but who was jilted by her.

> His death, which happened in his berth,
>   At forty-odd befell;
> They went and **told** the sexton, and
>   The sexton **tolled** the bell.

Notice that the words **told** and **tolled** are pronounced alike, though they are different in meaning and spelling.

Words which are pronounced alike but differ
in meaning are called HOMOPHONES.

A list of **homophones** appears on pages 106 and 107.

EXERCISE 129

Write the words which are pronounced like those below but which have a different meaning and spelling.

1. sun	6. gilt	11. hole	16. wood
2. die	7. rain	12. four	17. mist
3. flew	8. key	13. read	18. place
4. fowl	9. ring	14. paws	19. tied
5. higher	10. not	15. none	20. vain

EXERCISE 130

Rewrite this paragraph, using the correct words in place of those which are wrongly spelt.

Last weak Mother thought she wood like to go for a sale on the see. She herd that too boatmen had just maid there boat ready, so she went down to the key, where she did knot have to weight long, for the tied was write inn.

Homophones

Complete each of these sentences, choosing the correct word from those in brackets.

1. The children watched the —— taking off from the runway. (**plain; plane**)

2. We —— wet clothes to squeeze the water out of them. (**ring; wring**)

3. —— not, want not! (**waste; waist**)

4. The full-back had strained a —— and was unable to play. (**mussel; muscle**)

5. Judy asked for another —— of cake. (**piece; peace**)

6. We waited an —— for —— dinner. (**our; hour**)

7. Wilson had just eaten a large —— bun. (**currant; current**)

8. The horse's —— was plaited with gaily coloured ribbons. (**main; mane**)

9. Ann likes to —— every apple she eats. (**peal; peel**)

10. We took the shortest —— to London. (**root; route**)

Rewrite each sentence below, using the correct word in place of the one misspelt.

1. Joan of Arc was tied to a steak and burnt.

2. Eight men carried the beer at the colonel's funeral.

3. The children watched the little lambs gamble beside their mother.

4. There is an excellent cereal on television now.

5. The squirrel kept a horde of acorns buried under the leaves.

6. For lunch we had place and chips.

7. Some people prey every night and morning.

8. The champion fainted then landed a tremendous punch on his opponent's jaw.

9. The burglar had nerves of steal.

10. The old gentleman had a little hare on top of his head.

Homophones

Insert each pair of **homophones** correctly in the spaces in the following sentences.

1. The daring —— swam out to the —— which was moored some distance from the shore. (**buoy; boy**)
2. The grass on the race —— is rather ——. (**course; coarse**)
3. We shall have to buy a new —— for the boat before we advertise it for ——. (**sail; sale**)
4. The cross-country runner vaulted over the —— in fine ——. (**style; stile**)
5. Mother —— that Sandra had bought a —— dress. (**new; knew**)
6. Everyone started to —— as the full-back kicked the —— into the crowd. (**bawl; ball**)
7. The —— of both liners were tired after their long Mediterranean ——. (**cruise; crews**)
8. The —— of directors were —— by the chairman's long speech. (**bored; board**)
9. Spring is the —— to plant —— in the garden. (**thyme; time**)
10. The children told —— father that —— was a holiday on Friday. (**there; their**)

Complete each of these sentences, using a suitable pair of **homophones**.

Example: Janet —— Joan a bottle of violet ——.

Janet **sent** Joan a bottle of violet **scent**.

1. The Rovers —— the match by two goals to ——.
2. Harry —— down the country —— on his new pony.
3. Most people —— with their —— hand.
4. The grizzly —— climbed up into a —— tree.
5. Talking —— is not —— in class.
6. The customer paid by —— for his new —— suit.
7. The cowboy —— the hoofs of a large —— of cattle.
8. The new —— went upstairs and —— the beds.
9. The artist had never —— such a beautiful —— as the one he was painting.
10. The new —— is an improvement because it gives out —— heat with little coal.

Similes

as cold as ice

agile ....a monkey
alike ......two peas
bitter ......gall
black ......coal; pitch
blind ......a bat
bold ....brass
brave ......a lion
bright ....a button
brittle ....glass
brown ....a berry
busy ....a bee; an ant
clean ......a new pin
clear ......crystal
cool ....a cucumber
cunning ...a fox
dead ......a doornail
deaf ....a doorpost
dry ....a bone; dust
easy ....winking; ABC
fit ....a fiddle
flat ....a pancake
fresh ......a daisy
frisky ......a lamb
gentle ....a dove
graceful ...a swan
good ......gold
green ......grass
happy ....a lark; a king;
           a sandboy
hard ....iron; nails
heavy ......lead
hot ....fire
hungry ...a hunter
keen ....mustard
large ......life
light ....a feather
mad ....a hatter; a March Hare
meek ......a lamb
old ....the hills; Methuselah

as safe as houses

pale ....death
patient ...Job
plain ......a pikestaff
playful ...a kitten
pleased ...Punch
plump ....a partridge
poor ......a church mouse
proud ....a peacock
quick ....lightning
quiet ......a mouse
red ....a beetroot
rich ....Croesus
regular ...a clock; clockwork
right ......rain
round ....a barrel
sharp ....a razor
silent .....the grave
slippery ...an eel
slow ......a snail; a tortoise
smooth ...velvet
sober ....a judge
soft ....putty
sound ....a bell
sour ......vinegar
steady ....a rock
stiff ....a poker
straight ...an arrow; a ramrod
strong ....an ox; a horse; Samson
sweet ....honey; sugar
swift ......a hare; a deer
tender ....a chicken
thick ......thieves
thin ....a rake
timid ......a mouse
tough ....leather
warm ....toast
weak ......a kitten; water
wise ......an owl; Solomon
white ....snow

111

Similes

We often compare two things because they are similar in some particular way, though quite different in other respects.

Example: We may say that a certain man is **as strong as a horse.**

In appearance they are totally different, but both possess strength.

Such comparisons are called SIMILES. Study the list of similes on page 111, then work the following exercises.

EXERCISE 135

Write the **simile** which refers to each of these creatures.

EXERCISE 136

Give the **simile** connected with each of the following objects.

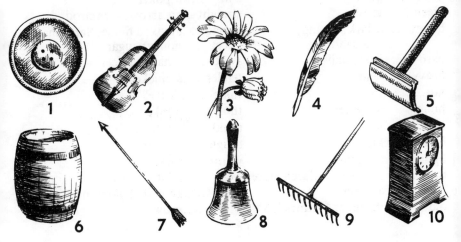

EXERCISE 137

Complete each sentence by using the correct **simile**.

1. The twins are as alike as ——.
2. The great hall was as silent as the ——.
3. The nurse in the children's ward was as patient as ——.
4. The inside-half was as slippery as an ——.
5. The big wardrobe was as steady as a ——.
6. This material is as smooth as ——.
7. These pears are as sweet as ——.
8. Martin found his homework as easy as ——.
9. The lemonade was as sour as ——.
0. After the attentions of his seconds the boxer was as right as ——.

EXERCISE 138

What are the missing words in these **similes**?

1. as bold as ....
2. as brown as a ....
3. as bitter as ....
4. as clean as a........
5. as dead as a ....
6. as cool as a ....
7. as dry as ....
8. as flat as a ....
9. as clear as ....
0. as good as ....

11. as .... as life
12. as .... as a lark
13. as .... as a hunter
14. as .... as a mule
15. as .... as an ox
16. as .... as mustard
17. as .... as a razor
18. as .... as houses
19. as .... as a doorpost
20. as .... as thieves

EXERCISE 139

Here are ten pairs of opposites. Write the **similes** which refer to ach pair.

Example: **bold**—as **bold** as **brass**

  timid—as **timid** as a **mouse**

1. black	2. hot	3. rich	4. hard	5. strong
white	cold	poor	soft	weak
6. slow	7. heavy	8. drunk	9. thin	10. tough
quick	light	sober	thick	tender

Proverbs

absence	Absence makes the heart grow fonder.
actions	Actions speak louder than words.
apple	An apple a day keeps the doctor away.

bed	As you make your bed so must you lie on it.
beggars	Beggars must not be choosers.
bed	Early to bed, early to rise,
	Makes a man healthy, wealthy and wise.

bird	A bird in the hand is worth two in the bush.
	The early bird catches the worm.
	Birds of a feather flock together.
bitten	Once bitten, twice shy.
blood	Blood is thicker than water.
	You cannot get blood out of a stone.
boys	Boys will be boys.
brooms	New brooms sweep clean.

cake	You cannot eat your cake and have it.
cat	A cat may look at a king.
	When the cat's away the mice will play.
charity	Charity begins at home.
chickens	Don't count your chickens until they are hatched.
cloud	Every cloud has a silver lining.
coat	Cut your coat according to your cloth.
cooks	Too many cooks spoil the broth.
courtesy	Courtesy costs nothing.

dog	Barking dogs seldom bite.
	Every dog has his day.
	Let sleeping dogs lie.
drowning	A drowning man will clutch at a straw.

eggs	Don't put all your eggs in one basket.
enough	Enough is as good as a feast.
example	Example is better than precept.
exchange	Exchange is no robbery.

feathers	Fine feathers make fine birds.
fire	Where there's smoke there's fire.
first	First come, first served.

Proverbs

fool	A fool and his money are soon parted.
fortune	Fortune knocks once at every man's door.
friend	A friend in need is a friend indeed.
fruit	Forbidden fruit tastes sweetest.
frying-pan	Out of the frying-pan into the fire.
God	God helps those who help themselves.
grasp	Grasp all, lose all.
habit	Habit is second nature.
hanged	As well be hanged for a sheep as a lamb.
haste	More haste, less speed.
hay	Make hay while the sun shines.
heads	Two heads are better than one.
heart	Faint heart never won fair lady.
honesty	Honesty is the best policy.
hunger	Hunger is the best sauce.
hungry	A hungry man is an angry man.
imitation	Imitation is the sincerest form of flattery.
lamb	A pet lamb is a cross ram.
late	Better late than never.
laugh	Laugh and grow fat.
	He laughs best who laughs last.
leak	A small leak will sink a great ship.
least	Least said soonest mended.
listeners	Listeners hear no good of themselves.
loaf	Half a loaf is better than no bread.
look	Look before you leap.
meat	One man's meat is another man's poison.
miss	A miss is as good as a mile.
necessity	Necessity is the mother of invention.
news	No news is good news.
pence	Look after the pence and the pounds will look after themselves.
penny	A penny saved is a penny gained.
	In for a penny, in for a pound.
	Penny wise, pound foolish.

Proverbs

piper	He who pays the piper calls the tune.
pitchers	Little pitchers have long ears.
port	Any port in a storm.
pot	Let not the pot call the kettle black.
practice	Practice makes perfect.
pride	Pride goes before a fall.
rohbing	Robbing Peter to pay Paul.
rod	Spare the rod and spoil the child.
sauce	What's sauce for the goose is sauce for the gander.
sight	Out of sight, out of mind.
smoke	Where there's smoke there's fire
stitch	A stitch in time saves nine.
stone	A rolling stone gathers no moss.
swallow	One swallow does not make a summer.
thief	Set a thief to catch a thief.
time	Time and tide wait for no man.
truth	Truth will out.
turn	One good turn deserves another.
twig	As the twig is bent so the tree's inclined.
vessels	Empty vessels make most noise.
waste	Waste not, want not.
water	We never miss the water till the well runs dry.
	Still waters run deep.
well	All's well that ends well.
	Leave well alone.
will	Where there's a will there's a way.
wind	It's an ill wind that blows nobody any good.
wine	When the wine's in the wit's out.
words	Fine words butter no parsnips.
work	All work and no play makes Jack a dull boy.
worth	What's worth doing is worth doing well.

Proverbs

> A PROVERB is a short, wise saying which has been in popular use for hundreds of years.

Some proverbs are easy to understand.

Examples: **Look before you leap.**

A fool and his money are soon parted.

But many proverbs are not so easy to understand.

Example: **Birds of a feather flock together.**

Actually, this refers not to birds but to people. It means that people mix with those who have tastes and interests similar to their own.

On pages 114–116 you will find a list of the commonest proverbs. You should try to learn these in preparation for the various tests on proverbs.

EXERCISE 140

Complete each of these unfinished **proverbs.**

1. All's well that —— ——.
2. Better late —— ——.
3. Exchange is —— ——.
4. First come, —— ——.
5. Once bitten, —— ——.
6. New brooms —— ——.
7. Penny wise, —— ——.
8. Still waters —— ——.
9. Great minds —— ——.
10. More haste, —— ——.

EXERCISE 141

Give the answers to these questions.

1. What should we do before leaping?
2. When should one make hay?
3. What is the mother of invention?
4. What kind of vessels make most noise?
5. What makes the heart grow fonder?
6. Where does charity begin?
7. What is the sincerest form of flattery?
8. What goes before a fall?
9. What will the mice do when the cat is away?
10. What does one good turn deserve?

Proverbs

Match the ten lettered **meanings** below with the ten numbered **proverbs.** Write numbers and letters only.

Example: 1. E

Proverbs

1. Don't put all your eggs in one basket.
2. A rolling stone gathers no moss.
3. One man's meat is another man's poison.
4. Make hay while the sun shines.
5. Empty vessels make most noise.
6. Cut your coat according to your cloth.
7. Birds of a feather flock together.
8. Every cloud has a silver lining.
9. Out of the frying-pan into the fire.
10. Don't count your chickens before they are hatched.

Meanings

A. People mix with those who have tastes similar to their own.
B. Live within your means.
C. It is unwise to reckon your gains until you actually get them.
D. Even when things seem gloomy there is always hope.
E. You should not risk all you have on a single speculation.
F. What suits one person may not suit another.
G. In trying to get yourself out of trouble you often get into a worse one.
H. It is the people who have nothing in their heads who talk most.
I. One who often changes his job will never be rich.
J. Work while you can; don't put things off till tomorrow.

Write the **proverbs** containing the following pairs of words.

1. cat — king
2. Enough — feast
3. Exchange — robbery
4. Hunger — sauce
5. Look — leap
6. smoke — fire
7. meat — poison
8. swallow — summer
9. sight — mind
10. goose — gander

Idioms

axe	to have an axe to grind (*to have something to gain by an action*)
bee	to have a bee in one's bonnet (*to be possessed by a crazy idea*)
belt	to hit below the belt (*to act unfairly towards a rival or an opponent*)
blanket	to be a wet blanket (*to be a spoilsport*)
bone	to have a bone to pick with someone (*to have a dispute to settle or a complaint to make*)
bow	to draw the long bow (*to exaggerate*)
breast	to make a clean breast of it (*to confess to some wrong*)
bull	to take the bull by the horns (*to meet difficulties or dangers boldly*)
canoe	to paddle one's own canoe (*to do things for oneself*)
cart	to put the cart before the horse (*to do things the wrong way round*)
cat	to let the cat out of the bag (*to disclose a secret*)
cloud	to be under a cloud (*to be under suspicion*)
Coventry	to send to Coventry (*to ignore and refuse to speak to a person*)
dark	to keep it dark (*to keep it secret*)
dog	to be a dog in the manger (*to deny to others what is useless to oneself*)
ends	to make both ends meet (*to live within one's means*)
feather	to have a feather in one's cap (*to have done something to be proud of*)
feather	to show the white feather (*to show cowardice*)
fence	to sit on the fence (*to refuse to take sides in a dispute*)
fiddle	to play second fiddle (*to take a back place while someone else leads*)

Idioms

hatchet	to bury the hatchet *(to settle a quarrel and live in peace)*
head	to hang one's head *(to be ashamed of oneself)*
hand	to live from hand to mouth *(to live only for today with no thought of tomorrow)*
horse	to ride the high horse *(to behave arrogantly; to be very haughty)*
horse	to flog a dead horse *(to do work which produces no results)*
iron	to strike while the iron is hot *(to act while conditions are favourable)*
lead	to swing the lead *(to dodge work by pretending to be ill)*
leaf	to turn over a new leaf *(to lead a new life)*
leave	to take French leave *(to go off without permission)*
loggerheads	to be at loggerheads *(to be quarrelling)*
mountain	to make a mountain out of a molehill *(to make trifling difficulties appear great ones)*
music	to face the music *(to take punishment or criticism without complaint)*
nest	to feather one's nest *(to add to one's possessions)*
nose	to pay through the nose *(to pay too high a price)*
p's and q's	to mind one's p's and q's *(to be careful how one behaves)*
rat	to smell a rat *(to be suspicious)*
shoulder	to give a person the cold shoulder *(to make him feel unwelcome)*
trumpet	to blow one's own trumpet *(to boast about oneself)*
water	to get into hot water *(to get into trouble)*
water	to throw cold water (on a suggestion) *(to discourage)*

Idioms

EXERCISE 144

Write the idiom illustrated by each of these pictures and give the meaning of each in your own words.

EXERCISE 145

Match these ten **idioms** with their **meanings,** writing numbers and letters only. *Example:* 1. F

Idioms

1. to bury the hatchet
2. to draw the long bow
3. to mind one's p's and q's
4. to let the cat out of the bag
5. to ride the high horse
6. to hit below the belt
7. to smell a rat
8. to paddle one's own canoe
9. to blow one's own trumpet
10. to be a wet blanket

Meanings

A. to be suspicious
B. to be very haughty
C. to be a spoilsport
D. to boast about oneself
E. to exaggerate
F. to make peace
G. to disclose a secret
H. to act unfairly
I. to be careful how one behaves
J. to do things for oneself

121

Idioms

Write the ten **idioms** indicated by these meanings.

1. to keep a matter secret
2. to pay far more for an article than it is really worth
3. to be constantly quarrelling with another person
4. to make someone feel that he is unwelcome and unwanted
5. to increase one's wordly possessions
6. to make difficulties appear very much more formidable than they actually are
7. to dodge work by shamming sickness
8. to discourage any suggested plan or idea
9. to ignore a person and refuse to speak to him
10. to have a dispute to settle with someone

EXERCISE 147

Complete each **idiom** below and give its meaning in your own words.

1. to live from hand to ——
2. to flog a dead ——
3. to have a —— in one's bonnet
4. to get into hot ——
5. to face the ——
6. to be under a ——
7. to turn over a new ——
8. to make a clean —— of it
9. to make both —— meet
10. to play —— fiddle

alive and kicking
bag and baggage
beck and call
body and soul
cats and dogs
chop and change
Darby and Joan
down and out
facts and figures
fair and square
fame and fortune
far and away
far and wide
fast and furious
fast and loose
fear and trembling
fire and water
first and foremost
fits and starts
flesh and blood
forgive and forget
free and easy
give and take
good and all
hale and hearty
hammer and tongs
hand and foot
hard and fast
hare and hounds
head and shoulders
heart and soul
heaven and earth
here and there
hide and seek
high and dry
high and low
hip and thigh
hither and thither
hue and cry
kith and kin

length and breadth
lock and key
long and short
might and main
neck and neck
off and on
one and all
out and about
over and above
over and done with
over and over
part and parcel
peace and plenty
rack and ruin
rank and file
root and branch
rough and ready
rough and tumble
round and round
safe and sound
short and sweet
sixes and sevens
slow and sure
spick and span
stuff and nonsense
sunshine and shadow
there and then
thick and thin
time and tide
tooth and nail
touch and go
tried and true
up and doing
ups and downs
watch and wait
ways and means
wear and tear
well and good
young and foolish

Twin Words

Complete each sentence below by using the other **twin word.**

1. The drunken lodger was turned out bag and ——.

2. The police found the shop till empty and the cashier bound hand and ——.

3. Mother keeps all her jewellery under lock and ——.

4. The old school had been allowed to go to rack and ——.

5. What the clerk said was all stuff and ——.

6. Although the house was a humble one it was quite spick and ——.

7. The team fought tooth and —— to reach the cup final.

8. We caught the plane to Paris but it was touch and ——.

9. We must think of ways and —— of raising funds to buy our new cricket equipment.

10. Although barely fourteen Michael is head and —— taller than his father.

Provide the missing word in each of these phrases.

1. kith and ——	11. —— and fortune
2. beck and ——	12. —— and easy
3. hammer and ——	13. —— and figures
4. fits and ——	14. —— and change
5. wear and ——	15. —— and sevens
6. slow and ——	16. —— and tumble
7. rank and ——	17. —— and sound
8. fair and ——	18. —— and furious
9. short and ——	19. —— and hearty
10. flesh and ——	20. —— and foolish

Twin Words

EXERCISE 150

Write the pair of **twin words** which could best be applied to each of the following.

Example: A man who has been bound so that he cannot move.

Answer: **hand and foot**

1. An old couple who have lived happily together for many years
2. A job tackled with a will
3. A crowd of people pursuing a pickpocket
4. A person who has no visible means of support
5. A youth who does silly things
6. Rain coming down in torrents
7. Two horses which are running dead level in a race
8. An old man who is remarkably healthy
9. A room which is spotlessly clean
10. A house which has been allowed to become dilapidated

EXERCISE 151

Complete each of these sentences by inserting both **twin words.**

1. I have told you —— and —— again not to walk on the flower beds.
2. The two comrades vowed to stick to each other through —— and ——.
3. He would move —— and —— to achieve his ambition.
4. The poor widow's income was barely enough to keep —— and —— together.
5. We searched —— and —— for the tennis ball but failed to find it.
6. Jim's parents have seen many —— and —— in their married life.
7. If you are satisfied with the results all —— and ——.
8. The young doctor was —— and —— in his work.
9. The —— and —— of the matter was that Tom Brown was punished for disobeying the school rules.
10. In our dealings with others we must learn to —— and ——.

125

Analogies

Just as a **young cat** is called a **kitten** so a **young sheep** is called a **lamb**.

A similarity of this kind is called an ANALOGY.

The above analogy can be expressed in this way:

cat is to kitten as sheep is to lamb

or   kitten is to cat as lamb is to sheep

Analogies may be based on homes, collective nouns, group names, diminutives, sounds, coverings, containers, etc.

EXERCISE 152

Complete these **analogies.**

1. **sheep** are to **flock** as **wolves** are to ....
2. **banana** is to **skin** as **orange** is to ....
3. **husband** is to **wife** as **king** is to ....
4. **water** is to **ice** as **liquid** is to ....
5. **inside** is to **outside** as **interior** is to ....
6. **uncle** is to **nephew** as **aunt** is to ....
7. **soldier** is to **squad** as **pupil** is to ....
8. **duck** is to **duckling** as **swan** is to ....
9. **food** is to **famine** as **water** is to ....
10. **dog** is to **paw** as **horse** is to ....

EXERCISE 153

Here is another way of making these comparisons. We may use : and :: in place of words.

1. rifle : bullet :: bow : ....
2. dog : puppy :: bear : ....
3. mother : daughter :: queen : ....
4. eye : sight :: nose : ....
5. train : station :: aeroplane : ....
6. out : in :: export : ....
7. hand : arm :: foot : ....
8. lion : animal :: wasp : ....
9. dish : fruit :: vase : ....
10. cobbler : shoes :: tailor : ....

Analogies

Insert the missing words.

1. **author** is to **book** as .... is to **statue**

2. **shoes** are to **feet** as .... are to **hands**

3. **feathers** are to **bird** as .... are to **fish**

4. **shell** is to **nut** as .... is to **cheese**

5. **dog** is to **kennel** as .... is to **lodge**

6. **speaker** is to **listener** as .... is to **pupil**

7. **coal** is to **scuttle** as .... is to **caddy**

8. **lion** is to **roar** as .... is to **trumpet**

9. **pilot** is to **plane** as .... is to **ship**

10. **up** is to **down** as .... is to **descend**

Complete each of these **analogies.**

1. **shopkeeper** is to **customer** as **doctor** is to ....

2. **foot** is to **toes** as **hand** is to ....

3. **composer** is to **music** as **poet** is to ....

4. **go** is to **went** as **do** is to ....

5. **conductor** is to **bus** as **guard** is to ....

6. **cow** is to **beef** as **pig** is to ....

7. **London** is to **England** as **Paris** is to ....

8. **fishmonger** is to **fish** as **florist** is to ....

9. **ship** is to **sea** as **aeroplane** is to ....

10. **revolver** is to **holster** as **sword** is to ....

127

Spelling

Complete each unfinished word in these sentences by adding **-able** or **-ible** as required.

1. The bill is pay—— on December 1st.
2. Donald was respons—— for locking the cupboards.
3. Early application for tickets is advis——.
4. Twelve is exactly divis—— by four.
5. Simon and Michael are insepar—— friends.
6. Pork is an indigest—— food.
7. Meat and fish are perish—— foods.
8. Beside the bed there was a revers—— rug.
9. The speaker's voice was almost inaud——.
10. People are often irrit—— when they are ill.

Complete each word by inserting **a**, **e**, or **o** as necessary.

1. burgl*r	6. radiat*r	11. councill*r	16. corrid*r
2. bugl*r	7. cell*r	12. report*r	17. regul*r
3. cobbl*r	8. popul*r	13. pill*r	18. dock*r
4. tail*r	9. decorat*r	14. regist*r	19. doct*r
5. gramm*r	10. begg*r	15. bachel*r	20. schol*r

In each sentence below complete the word from which letters have been omitted.

1. The second month of the year is Feb – – – – y.
2. In some schools the boys and girls are in sep – – – te classes.
3. When you pay a bill see that you get a re – – – – t.
4. Susan's new ad – – – – s is 14 High Street, Gleeville.
5. The day after Tuesday is W – – – – – day.
6. Janet borrows a book from the school lib – – – y every week.
7. Several articles of jew – – – – – y, including a diamond ring, were stolen from the flat.
8. The Duke paid a s – – pri – e visit to the camp yesterday.
9. The sec – – – – – y had to deal with all the correspondence of the office.
10. The hotel has ac – – m – – dation for a hundred guests.

Spelling

EXERCISE 159

Rewrite this paragraph, substituting **ie** or **ei** for the asterisks in he incomplete words.

Last week as my n**ce and her boy fr**nd, Martin, were strolling n a f**ld near Manor Farm they heard a w**rd noise coming from he barn. Bel**ving that a th**f for whom the police were searching vas hiding there, Marting s**zed a thick p**ce of wood from a wood ile entered the barn and forced the hunted man to y**ld.

EXERCISE 160

In each line below one word is wrongly spelt. Write these words orrectly in a column numbered 1 to 10.

1. spacious	hidious	curious	tedious
2. intense	immense	commense	nonsense
3. grocer	draper	waiter	traiter
4. ornament	goverment	tournament	testament
5. jestor	ancestor	inventor	sculptor
6. Wednesday	Saterday	Tuesday	Thursday
7. necessary	military	cemetary	temporary
8. wintery	gallery	cookery	scullery
9. liberate	operate	separate	favourate
10. intention	extention	attention	detention

EXERCISE 161

Each missing word in these sentences contains a silent letter, ;, **k, l, p, r** or **w**. Make a list of the complete words.

1. After the storm the sea became quite ****.
2. The old gipsy's face was lined with ********.
3. Rabbits cause damage by ****ing the trunks of young trees.
4. George hurt his ******** when he rapped on the door.
5. The ship drifted onto the rocks and became a total *****.
6. Susan has ******* a lovely jumper for her mother.
7. By attending school you increase your store of ********.
8. ******* clothes makes them smooth after washing.
9. The church choir chanted the twenty-third *****.
0. ********* tyres are filled with air.

Words within Words

By rearranging some of the letters in the word

SEPARATE

we can make other words.
Examples: **spear; spare; pears; rates; stare; steep,** etc.

EXERCISE 162

In a similar way use the letters of each word in capitals below to form words which correspond to the meanings given.

A.   **PREPARATORY**

1. Very uncommon
2. A talking bird
3. A man who traps wild animals
4. The Head of the Roman Catholic Church
5. The Christmas ***** was held in school.

B.   **COMPENSATION**

1. To bend forward
2. Not shut
3. To bring one's foot down with force
4. The dishonest servant was given a month's ******.
5. Never board a bus whilst it is in ******.

C.   **DENOMINATOR**

1. The man who digs our coal from the earth
2. The opposite of **outer**
3. Another word for **midday**
4. Animals in circuses are ******* to perform clever tricks.
5. The engine that drives a car

D.   **DISCOURAGEMENT**

1. A desire for more than one's share
2. To rub out
3. A small river or a large brook
4. To whip severely
5. The part of a flower containing the pollen

Words within Words

All the words except one in each of the lines below can be formed from the letters in the word in capitals. Write the odd word in each line. Each letter may be used only once.

1.   **INDISCREET**

credit   erect   street   cried   steer   trees

2.   **CONSISTENTLY**

silent   style   scent   costly   sister   scones

3.   **PARADISE**

praise   draper   parade   pride   spire   spider

4.   **FORTNIGHT**

fright   throng   thing   tonight   tight   nought

5.   **ENDEAVOUR**

rounder   drove   devour   vendor   endure   round

6.   **DISREPUTABLE**

bleat   petal   brute   stable   steep   tablet

7.   **CREATURE**

cruet   trace   curate   truce   centre   create

8.   **IMPERTINENT**

temper   inert   intent   mitten   repent   invent

9.   **ADMINISTRATION**

strain   station   mansion   strong   rations   storm

Abbreviations

A.A.	Automobile Association	g	gram
A.B.	Able-bodied seaman	G.C.	George Cross
A.D.	In the year of Our Lord	Gen.	General
a.m.	before noon	G.M.	George Medal
Apr.	April	G.M.T.	Greenwich Mean Time
Aug.	August	G.P.O.	General Post Office
Ave.	Avenue		
A.1	First class	H.M.	Her Majesty
		H.M.S.	Her Majesty's Ship
b.	born	Hon. Sec.	Honorary Secretary
B.A.	Bachelor of Arts	h.p.	horse power
B.B.C.	British Broadcasting Corporation		hire purchase
B.C.	Before Christ	H.R.H.	His (Her) Royal Highne
B.R.	British Rail		
B.Sc.	Bachelor of Science	i.e.	that is
B.S.T.	British Summer Time	inst.	this month
		I.O.U.	I owe you
cc	cubic centimetre		
cg	centigram	Jan.	January
C.I.D.	Criminal Investigation Department	J.P.	Justice of the Peace
cl	centilitre	Jun.	Junior
cm	centimetre		
C.O.D.	Cash on Delivery	kg	kilogram
Co.	Company	km	kilometre
c/o	care of	km/h	kilometres per hour
Col.	Colonel	k.o.	knock-out
Cons.	Conservative		
Cr.	Credit	l	litre
Cresc.	Crescent	lat.	latitude
		l.b.w.	leg before wicket
Dept.	Department	Lib.	Liberal
dm	decimetre		
dg	decigram	m	metre
dl	decilitre	m.	married
do.	ditto—the same	M.A.	Master of Arts
doz.	dozen	Mar.	March
Dr.	Doctor; Debtor	max.	maximum
		M.B.	Bachelor of Medicine
e.g.	for example	M.B.E.	Member of the Order the British Empire
E.R.	Queen Elizabeth		
Esq.	Esquire	M.C.	Military Cross
Est.	Established		
etc.	and other things		
Feb.	February		

M.C.	Master of Ceremonies		R.A.C.	Royal Automobile Club
M.D.	Doctor of Medicine		R.A.F.	Royal Air Force
Messrs.	Messieurs (French) sirs		R.C.	Roman Catholic
M.F.H.	Master of the Foxhounds		Rd.	Road
min.	minimum		Rev.	Reverend
min.	minute		R.I.P.	May he (she) rest in peace
ml	millilitre		R.N.	Royal Navy
mm	millimetre		R.S.P.C.A.	Royal Society for the Prevention of Cruelty to Animals
M.O.H.	Medical Officer of Health			
Mr.	Mister		R.S.V.P.	Reply if you please
Mrs.	Mistress (married woman)		Rt. Hon.	Right Honourable
N.B.	Note well		Sec. Mod.	Secondary Modern
No.	Number		Sen.	Senior
Nov.	November		Sept.	September
N.S.P.C.C.	National Society for the Prevention of Cruelty to Children		Soc.	Socialist
			Sq.	Square
			St.	Saint; Street
O.B.E.	Officer of the Order of the British Empire		T.A.	Territorial Army
			T.B.	Tuberculosis
Oct.	October		Tel.	Telephone; Telegraph
O.H.M.S.	On Her Majesty's Service		Terr.	Terrace
O.K.	Correct		T.T.	Teetotaller
				Tuberculin Tested (milk)
p.	page			
p.a.	per annum		U.K.	United Kingdom
P.C.	Police Constable		U.N.O.	United Nations Organisation
p.c.	postcard			
p.m.	afternoon		ult.	last month
P.O.	Post Office		U.S.A.	United States of America
	Postal Order		U.S.S.R.	Union of Soviet Socialist Republics
P.S.	Postscript			
P.T.	Physical Training		v.	versus (against)
P.T.O.	Please Turn Over		V.C.	Victoria Cross
			via	by way of
			V.I.P.	Very Important Personage
			viz.	namely
Q.C.	Queen's Counsellor		Y.M.C.A.	Young Men's Christian Association

Abbreviations

To save time certain words and phrases are written in a shortened form. If you look at a calendar you will see that the names of the days are not printed in full, but like this:

Sun.　　Mon.　　Tues.　　Wed.　　Thurs.　　Fri.　　Sat.

These shortened forms are called ABBREVIATIONS.

You are already familiar with some abbreviations. In arithmetic you write **p** for **penny** or **pence, cm** for **centimetre, g** for **gram, l** for **litre,** and so on.

History tells us that Julius Caesar invaded Britain in 55 **B.C.** and that the Battle of Hastings was fought in **A.D.** 1066.

In addressing letters we may use such abbreviations as **Mr., Mrs., Dr., Rev., Col.,** etc.

Professional men use letters to show their qualifications, e.g. **M.A., D.D., Mus. Bac., M.D.,** etc.

It is important to know the meanings of the commonest of the abbreviations, a list of which will be found on pages 132 and 133. Learn as many of these as you can, then work the exercises which appear below. If there are any you cannot do, refer to the list.

EXERCISE 164

Give the meanings of the **abbreviations** which are printed in heavy type in these sentences.

1. The Arsenal **v.** Everton match ended in a draw.

2. I will send you a **p.c.** next Tuesday.

3. The letter was addressed to John Milton, **Esq.**

4. P. May . . . **c** Harvey . . . **b** Lindwall.

5. Uncle Ron drove his 10 **h.p.** veteran car to Brighton.

6. He told us it could do 70 **km/h**

7. William Shakespeare, **b.** 1564, **d.** 1616.

8. The poem will be found on **p.** 26.

9. Frank Scott, **c/o** Mrs. North, High Street, New Town.

10. Christopher saw **H.M.S.** Eagle at Portsmouth.

Abbreviations

EXERCISE 165

What do the **abbreviations** in these sentences stand for?

1. My uncle works at the B.B.C.
2. The M.O.H. visited the school yesterday.
3. I will write to the G.P.O. about the lost parcel.
4. Goods will be sent C.O.D. if desired.
5. The purpose of U.N.O. is to safeguard world peace.
6. The collision occurred at 15.45 G.M.T.
7. Henry Tilling, Ltd. Est. 1789.
8. An A.A. patrol came to our rescue.
9. The cruel parents were reported to the N.S.P.C.C.
10. Mr. Simpkins has been appointed a J.P.

EXERCISE 166

The **abbreviations** in this exercise are from Latin.

1. The powder will kill beetles, ants, cockroaches, **etc.**
2. We travelled from Cardiff to London **via** the Severn Tunnel.
3. The secretary gets a salary of £12 000 **p.a.**
4. Thank you for your letter of the 14th **inst.**
5. **P.S.** I have found the purse I lost.
6. **N.B.** Children under 14 will not be admitted.
7. The dispatch case bore the letters **E.R.**
8. They were short of two things, **viz.** time and money.
9. Fire destroyed much of London in 1666 **A.D.**
10. School commences at 9 **a.m.**

EXERCISE 167

Here are some cricket fixtures. Write the names of the counties in full.

Championship Table	Minor Counties
1. Worcs. v. Kent	6. Wilts. v. Cambs.
2. Notts. v. Hants.	7. Lincs. v. Bucks.
3. Essex v. Glam.	8. Berks. v. Staffs.
4. Yorks. v. Surrey	9. Beds. v. Suffolk
5. Lancs. v. Glos.	10. Herts. v. Cornwall

Rhymes

In poetry the words at the end of certain lines **rhyme,** that is, the last part of each of them sounds alike.

Examples: **hat** rhymes with **mat**
heat rhymes with **meat**
shade rhymes with **blade**

Sometimes the spelling of the rhyming portions differs.

Examples: **rest** rhymes with **breast**
deed rhymes with **bead**
leaf rhymes with **chief**
write rhymes with **bright**

EXERCISE 168

Each of these lines contain rhyming words. Add two more rhyming words to each line.

1.	hard	card	guard	....	....
2.	pair	mare	wear	....	....
3.	date	wait	great	....	....
4.	buy	cry	sigh	....	....
5.	must	crust	dust	....	....
6.	coat	note	float	....	....
7.	brain	plane	reign	....	....
8.	sleigh	stay	prey	....	....
9.	breed	plead	recede	....	....
10.	clean	green	machine	....	....

EXERCISE 169

Each line below contains three rhyming words from which certain letters are missing. Complete each word, bearing in mind that different letters can sometimes be used to make rhyming words.

1.	**ean	**een	**ene
2.	**ear	**eer	***ere
3.	*urt	**irt	**ert
4.	*ore	*our	*oar
5.	*oal	*ole	*owl
6.	*urse	*erse	*orse
7.	*erk	*ork	**irk
8.	**um	*ome	**umb
9.	*oam	*ome	*omb
10.	*oes	*ows	*ose

136

EXERCISE 170

Write this verse of poetry, inserting the words below in their correct places.

plain	battle	eye	rain
by	ditches	cattle	witches

Faster than fairies, faster than ——
Bridges and houses, hedges and ——;
And charging along like troops in a ——,
All through the meadows the horses and ——;
All of the sights of the hill and the ——
Fly as thick as driving ——;
And, ever again, in the wink of an ——
Painted stations whistle ——.

EXERCISE 171

Fit these five pairs of rhyming words into their proper places in the ten lines of poetry which follow.

| spray | best | cheery | light | snow |
| day | rest | aweary | night | blow |

Into the sunshine, full of the ——,
Leaping and flashing from morn till ——!
Into the moonlight, whiter than ——,
Waving so flower-like when the winds ——!
Into the starlight, rushing in ——,
Happy at midnight, happy by ——!
Ever in motion, blithesome and ——,
Still climbing heavenward, never ——;
Glad of all weathers, still seeming ——,
Upward or downward motion thy ——.

EXERCISE 172

Write each of these as four lines of poetry.

A. I wandered lonely as a cloud that floats on high o'er vales and hills, when all at once I saw a crowd, a host of golden daffodils.

B. Fair is the land of hill and plain, and lonesome dells in misty mountains; and crags where eagles in tempest reign, and swan-loved lakes and fountains.

Homes

a badger **lives in a** sett

bear	den
beaver	lodge
bee	hive
bird	nest
bishop	palace
convict	prison
dog	kennel
dove	dovecote
eagle	eyrie
fox	lair, earth
hare	form
horse	stable
king (queen)	palace
lumberjack	log cabin
lion	den
minister	manse
mouse	hole, nest

a monk **lives in a** monastery

nun	convent, nunnery
otter	holt
parson	parsonage
pig	sty
prisoner	cell
rabbit (tame)	hutch
rabbit (wild)	burrow, warren
rector	rectory
sheep	fold, pen
snail	shell
soldier	barracks, camp
spider	web
squirrel	drey
tiger	lair
wasp	nest
vicar	vicarage

EXERCISE 173

What are the **homes** of the following called?

1. a king
2. a mouse
3. a wild rabbit
4. a bear
5. a snail
6. an otter
7. a horse
8. a prisoner
9. a spider
10. a squirrel
11. a wasp
12. a hare
13. a rector
14. a nun
15. a lion
16. a tiger
17. a vicar
18. a sheep
19. a badger
20. a parson

EXERCISE 174

Write each sentence below, filling in the name of the **home** of the creature mentioned.

1. A dog's —— should be waterproof and raised above the ground level.
2. The large —— contained a fat sow and her ten piglets.
3. Hiawatha knew where the beavers built their ——.
4. The otter's —— is a hole tunnelled in the bank of a river.
5. Geoffrey has made a fine —— for his pet rabbits.
6. The eagle had built its —— high up among the rocks.
7. The —— of a hare is just a flattened space in the grass.
8. Several doves had alighted on the roof of their ——.
9. Peel's "View halloo!" would awaken the dead, or the fox from his —— in the morning.
10. The badger lives in a hole in the earth called a ——.

EXERCISE 175

Insert in each sentence the name of the **dwelling** of the person mentioned.

1. Although roughly built the lumberjack's —— was warm and dry.
2. The regiment marched to its ——, a huge stone building just outside the town.
3. A —— is the home of religious women.
4. The Baptist minister's —— was situated next to the church.
5. The —— on the island had been built by Franciscan monks.
6. In the afternoon several of the clergy were entertained at the Bishop's ——.
7. Most of the convicts in the —— were serving long sentences.

Diminutives

Adult	Young	Adult	Young
bear	cub	hare	leveret
cat	kitten	hen	chick
cow	calf	human	child; baby
deer	fawn	lion	cub
dog	puppy	mare	filly
duck	duckling	owl	owlet
eagle	eaglet	pig	piglet
eel	elver	sheep	lamb
elephant	calf	stallion	colt
frog	tadpole	swan	cygnet
goat	kid	whale	calf
goose	gosling		

EXERCISE 176

Insert the correct **diminutive** in each sentence below.

1. The cat carried the —— gently by its neck.
2. Nine lively —— were ranged round the sleeping sow.
3. When the sheep bleated the —— ran to her at once.
4. The mother bear will defend her —— with her life.
5. During the night Daisy, the Jersey cow, gave birth to a ——.
6. The goose hissed when Jill tried to pick up one of her ——.
7. The teacher said that the —— would soon grow into frogs.
8. One of the fluffy little —— had climbed on to the mother hen's back.
9. The little —— could not keep up with the nanny-goat.
10. The duck was swimming down the river followed by several of her ——.
11. The chestnut mare cantered round the field followed by Sandra, her ——.
12. The eel which is found in British rivers begins life as a tiny —— in the Atlantic Ocean.
13. A —— is not as white as a fully-grown swan.
14. There were four hungry —— in the eagle's nest.
15. The —— which was with the red deer was three months old.

Sounds

Creature	Sound	Object	Sound
apes	gibber	anvil	clang
bears	growl	bagpipes	skirl
bees	hum	bell	tinkle; peal
beetles	drone	bow	twang
bulls	bellow	brakes	grind
cats	mew; meow; purr	bugle	call
cockerels	crow	bullet	ping
cows	low; moo	cane	whack; swish
crows	caw	chains	jangle; rattle
dogs	bark; growl	clock	tick
donkeys	bray	coins	clink; jingle
doves	coo	corks	pop
ducks	quack	dishes	rattle; clatter
elephants	trumpet	door	slam; bang
frogs	croak	drum	beat
geese	cackle; hiss	engine	throb; splutter
hens	cluck; cackle	explosion	blast
horses	neigh; whinny	feet	tramp; shuffle
hounds	bay	gun	boom
hyenas	laugh; scream	hinges	creak
lambs	bleat	hoofs	thunder; clatter
lions	roar	horn	toot
monkeys	chatter	kettle	singing
mice	squeak	leaves	rustle
owls	hoot	paper	rustle; crackle
oxen	low	raindrops	patter
parrots	screech; talk	rifle	report
pigs	squeal; grunt	saw	buzz
pigeons	coo	silk	rustle
rabbits	squeal	siren	wail
robins	chirp	skirts	swish
sheep	bleat	steam	hiss
snakes	hiss	stream	babble; murmer
sparrows	chirp	thunder	peal; clap
swallows	twitter	train	rumble
turkeys	gobble	whip	lash; crack
wolves	howl	whistle	shriek
wrens	warble	wings	whirr

Sounds

In each space below insert the name of the **noise** made by the creature mentioned.

1. The snake —— and made a lunge at the man's feet.
2. The children were awakened by the —— of mice behind the skirting boards of their bedroom.
3. As the tiger snarled the elephant —— loudly and prepared for the attack.
4. The little pig —— as the farmer seized hold of him.
5. When the sheep —— her two little lambs came running to her.
6. The villagers could hear the —— of a large pack of wolves in the nearby forest.
7. Several monkeys were —— excitedly as they swung from tree to tree.
8. Large numbers of rooks were —— together as the building of the rookery went on.
9. The Persian cat —— with contentment as it lazed in the warmth of the fire.
10. From the ruins of the castle came the —— of owls.

Insert the correct **noise** or **animal** in each space below.

1. hounds	....	11.	croak
2. swallows	....	12.	neigh
3. geese	....	13.	bray
4. turkeys	....	14.	cluck
5. bears	....	15.	bellow
6. parrots	....	16.	laugh
7. cockerels	....	17.	hum
8. oxen	....	18.	drone
9. robins	....	19.	gibber
10. doves	....	20.	roar

Sounds

EXERCISE 179

Complete each sentence by giving the correct **sound.**

1. The room was so quiet that the —— of the clock could plainly be heard.
2. The burglar's presence was betrayed by the —— of the rusty door hinges.
3. Colin awoke to the —— of raindrops against his bedroom window.
4. The firemen raced towards their engine as the siren ——.
5. A loud —— of thunder warned the picnickers to take shelter from the approaching storm.
6. With a —— of the whistle the train entered the tunnel.
7. The approach of the Highland regiment was heralded by the —— of bagpipes.
8. There was a loud —— of wings as the large flock of starlings flew up into the air.
9. The huntsmen rode through the village with a —— of hoofs.
10. The shrill —— of a bugle summoned the troops to parade.

EXERCISE 180

Insert the correct word in each phrase below.

1. the .... of an anvil
2. the .... of a drum
3. the .... of a cane
4. the .... of a train
5. the .... of a kettle
6. the .... of corks
7. the .... of brakes
8. the .... of skirts
9. the .... of leaves
10. the .... of chains
11. the jingle of ....
12. the ping of a· ....
13. the boom of a ....
14. the shuffling of ....
15. the twang of a ....
16. the toot of a ....
17. the buzz of a ....
18. the report of a ....
19. the hissing of ....
20. the crack of a ....

143

Occupations

acrobat	Performs tricks on the trapeze, turns handsprings, etc.
announcer	Introduces radio and television programmes.
architect	Designs buildings and supervises their erection.
artist	Draws and paints pictures.
auctioneer	Sells goods to the highest bidder.
athlete	Excels in outdoor games and sports.
barber	Shaves or trims beards and cuts hair.
blacksmith	Makes articles of iron.
cabinet-maker	Makes various articles of furniture.
caddie	Carries a golfer's clubs, finds the ball, etc.
carpenter	Works in wood, especially in building.
cashier	Takes the money in a shop, restaurant, etc.
charwoman	Does housework for payment by the hour.
chauffeur	Employed to drive a private motor-car.
chef	An expert male cook.
chemist	Sells medicines, pills, ointments, etc.
clothier	Sells various articles of clothing.
cobbler	Repairs boots and shoes.
collier	Digs coal from the earth.
conductor	(a) Beats time for an orchestra or choir.
	(b) Collects fares on a bus or tram.
confectioner	Makes or sells sweets.
cooper	Makes barrels and casks.
cutler	Makes knives, forks, scissors, razors, etc.
decorator	Paints and papers rooms.
dentist	Fills and extracts teeth; supplies artificial teeth.
detective	Investigates crimes.
dustman	Collects the rubbish from houses.
engineer	Looks after engines.
explorer	Travels in order to make discoveries.
farrier	A blacksmith who shoes horses.
fishmonger	Sells fish.
florist	Grows or sells flowers for a living.
fruiterer	Sells fruit and vegetables.
gamekeeper	Looks after game and prevents poaching.
glazier	Fits glass into windows.
greengrocer	Sells fruit and vegetables.
grocer	Sells butter, cheese, bacon, tea, etc.
herbalist	Sells herbs and herbal remedies.

hosier	Sells stockings, socks and underwear.
ironmonger	Sells tools, nails, screws, etc.
jeweller	Deals in or sets precious stones, sells watches, etc.
jockey	Rides horses in races as a profession.
journalist	Writes articles for newspapers, journals, etc.
judge	An official appointed to preside over a law-court.
lawyer	An expert in the practice of the law.
librarian	One in charge of a library.
mason	A person whose work is building with stone.
mechanic	One skilled in the use of machinery.
milliner	Makes or sells ladies' hats.
navvy	Labourer employed in heavy work such as road-repairing.
newsagent	Sells newspapers and journals.
novelist	Writes novels.
optician	Makes or sells spectacles; tests eyesight.
photographer	Takes photographs.
pilot	(a) Takes ships into or out of harbour.
	(b) Controls an aeroplane.
plumber	Fits and repairs water pipes.
porter	(a) Railway servant who handles luggage.
	(b) Doorkeeper.
poulterer	Sells geese, ducks, turkeys, etc.
referee	Sees the rules are obeyed in football, boxing, etc.
reporter	Writes reports of events for the press.
saddler	Makes and repairs saddles and harnesses.
sculptor	Carves or models figures in stone, marble, etc.
shepherd	Looks after sheep.
shipwright	Builds or repairs ships.
stationer	Sells writing paper, envelopes, postcards, etc.
steeplejack	Repairs tall chimneys, steeples, towers, etc.
stevedore	Loads and unloads ships.
stoker	Looks after a furnace or the fire of a steam engine.
surgeon	Performs surgical operations.
tinker	Mends pots and pans.
tobacconist	Sells tobacco, cigarettes, pipes, etc.
typist	Types letters, etc. on a typewriter.
umpire	Sees the rules are obeyed in cricket and other games.
undertaker	Arranges and manages funerals.
watchmaker	Makes and repairs watches.

Occupations

Write the names of the **occupations** shown in the pictures below.

EXERCISE 182

Name the **occupations** of the people who sell:

1. pork, beef, mutton, etc.
2. hake, cod, herrings, etc.
3. apples, pears, plums, etc.
4. sweets and chocolates
5. clothing of various kinds

6. tobacco and cigarettes
7. flowers, wreaths, bouquets, etc.
8. medicines, ointments, etc.
9. flour, cheese, bacon, etc.
10. writing paper, envelopes, etc.

146

Occupations

Complete each sentence by using the name of the **occupation** indicated.

1. I could not buy the right kind of screw from the ——.
2. After sawing the wood the —— planed it to make it smooth.
3. The —— had great difficulty in extracting Wilson's teeth.
4. George has gone to his —— to be measured for a new suit.
5. The —— was in his studio working on a new painting.
6. After taking Jill's temperature the —— ordered her to stay in bed.
7. The —— promised to repair David's shoes by Friday.
8. Perched on top of the tall factory chimney the —— was carrying out repairs.
9. The —— who performed the operation is the cleverest in the country.
10. The —— did not take long to repair the leak in the water pipe.

Name the **occupation** of one who:

1. carves statues
2. looks after sheep
3. fixes glass in windows
4. flies an aeroplane
5. shaves men
6. drives his employer's car
7. makes and sells ladies' hats
8. carries a golfer's bag
9. arranges funerals
10. mends pots and pans

What are these people likely to be:

1. Horatio Collingwood, A.B.
2. Sir Frederick Milne, M.D.
3. Sir Joseph Watkins, Q.C.
4. Mr. Peter Walcott, L.D.S.
5. P.C. Havard
6. Lawrence Gibbon, M.P.S.
7. Sir James Keyes, C.I.D.
8. William Harford, R.A.
9. Walter Welling, F.R.C.O.
10. Rev. G. H. Cooper, B.D.

Occupations

What's My Line?

1. I take the money at a large restaurant.
2. I look after a large public building.
3. I sell newspapers, journals, magazines, etc.
4. I carry passengers' bags at the railway station.
5. I gather news for the Daily Recorder.
6. I design buildings and draw plans of them.
7. I travel about selling goods for a large firm.
8. I make saddles and harnesses for horses.
9. I try to discover who committed a crime.
10. I sell cabbages, potatoes, turnips, etc.

People

ancestor	A person from whom one is descended.
assassin	A hired murderer.
bachelor	An unmarried man.
bankrupt	Is unable to pay his debts.
blackleg	Goes to work whilst his mates are on strike.
cannibal	Eats human flesh
conscript	One compelled by law to serve with the Forces.
cynic	Sneers at others, believing their motives selfish.
eavesdropper	Listens to conversation not intended for his ears.
emigrant	Leaves his native land to live abroad.
exile	One banished from his native country.
glutton	Eats more than is good for him.
hermit	Forsakes others to live entirely by himself.
host	Entertains people at his house.
hypocrite	Pretends to be better than he really is.
immigrant	Comes into a country to settle there.
impostor	Tries to make people think he is somebody else.
martyr	Suffers death for the beliefs he holds.
mimic	Imitates the voice and actions of others.
miser	Lives sparingly in order to hoard money.
optimist	Always looks on the bright side of life.
orphan	A child whose parents are dead.
patriot	Serves his country loyally because he loves it.
pedestrian	Travels about on foot.
pessimist	Looks on the gloomy side of life.
philanthropist	Shows his love for mankind by practical help.
pilgrim	Travels to a sacred place as a religious devotion.
prophet	Foretells coming events.
renegade	A deserter from a religious faith or political party.
scapegoat	Takes the blame for the misdoings of others.
spendthrift	Spends money unnecessarily.
spinster	An unmarried woman.
stowaway	Hides on a ship, etc. to avoid paying the fare.
traitor	Betrays his country, or any trust.
truant	Pupil absent from school without permission.
tyrant	Uses his power to oppress others.
vegetarian	Eats no meat; lives on vegetables, fruit, etc.
volunteer	Offers to serve of his own free will.
wiseacre	Pretends to be very wise.

People

What word is used for a person who:

1. sells his country's secrets to a foreign power?
2. habitually gets drunk?
3. hides aboard a ship in order to get a free passage?
4. travels to a sacred place as a religious duty?
5. would sacrifice his life rather than give up his religious beliefs?
6. is compelled to serve in the Army, Navy or Air Force?
7. lives all by himself, far from the dwellings of others?
8. eats the flesh of human beings?
9. makes himself out to be much better than he actually is?
10. listens at keyholes to hear what others are saying?

EXERCISE 188

Write, in a column, the surnames which begin these sentences; then opposite each write the word which fits the person.

Example: **Kenyon** was made to shoulder the blame for the misdeeds of others.

Answer: **Kenyon —— scapegoat**

1. **Austin** owes £976 and has only £1·75 to his name.
2. **Bell** worked in the factory when his mates were out on strike.
3. **Cook** is always bright and cheerful, and is never downhearted.
4. **Dawson** is too mean to buy enough food for himself although he is a very rich man.
5. **Evans** is a man who has never been married.
6. **Farley** eats as much as three ordinary men put together.
7. **Grey** spends large sums of money buying things he will never want.
8. **Hawkins** never eats any meat, his diet consisting chiefly of fruit and vegetables.
9. **Ingram** loves England and would die to defend it if necessary.
10. **Jenkins** sails for New Zealand tomorrow and intends to make his home there.

Describing People

The ability to write clear and accurate descriptions of people is a most desirable accomplishment. If you read good books you will find they contain many excellent descriptions of real and imaginary persons which are well worth studying.

Consider the following description of the Artful Dodger, which is taken from *Oliver Twist.*

"He was a snub-nosed, flat-browed, common-faced boy enough; and as dirty a juvenile as one would wish to see; but he had about him all the airs and manners of a man. He was short for his age; with rather bow-legs, and little, sharp ugly eyes. He wore a man's coat which reached nearly to his heels. He had turned the cuffs back, half-way up his arm, to get his hands out of his sleeves, apparently with the ultimate view of thrusting them into the pockets of his corduroy trousers; for there he kept them."

Notice that Dickens has told his readers something about the Dodger's **build, forehead, eyes, nose, clothes, habits** and **manners.**

And this is Stevenson's description of Long John Silver, that unforgettable character in *Treasure Island.*

"His left leg was cut off close to the hip, and under the left shoulder he carried a crutch, which he managed with wonderful dexterity, hopping about on it like a bird. He was very tall and strong, with a face as big as a ham—plain and pale, but intelligent and smiling."

When writing a description of a person you should mention first of all the most prominent features, such as Silver's stump and crutch, or the Dodger's bandy legs.

You probably know many people whom you could describe in a very interesting way. You may perhaps remember Tom by his snub nose, Jack by his curly hair, Bill by his high forehead, Dick by his irregular teeth, Mary by her clear, blue eyes, Molly by her dimpled cheeks, Susie by her long, brown plaits, Janet by her shrill voice, and so on.

Many of these have certain little habits by which they can be identified. Bill is constantly blinking his eyes, Patricia is always tossing her head to get her hair behind her shoulders, Margaret has a permanent pout, Jack frequently shrugs his shoulders, and so on.

Describing People

In writing your descriptions pay attention to the following points. Make a list of these describing words in your notebook.

Figure: tall, short, lanky, stout, thin, frail, delicate, athletic, muscular, weedy, erect, bent, sturdy, lusty, stalwart, drooping, robust, brawny, husky, manly, powerful strapping, gigantic, deformed

Face and head: round, oval, long, small, square-jawed, thin, fat, bullet, flat, wrinkled, wizened

Forehead: narrow, flat, bulging, receding, wrinkled, wide, prominent, high

Nose: long, flat, bulging, snub, straight broad, dainty, enormous, bulbous, aquiline (eagle-like)

Hair: straight, wavy, curly, matted, unkempt, coarse, fine, tangled, brown, grey, silvery, auburn, golden, long, silky, shingled, bobbed, plaited

Eyes: clear, bright, large, small, brown, blue, grey, sly, merry, beady, shifty, twinkling, sparkling, round, almond-shaped

Skin: pale, swarthy, tanned, dusky, fair, bronzed, sunburnt, florid, ruddy, rough, smooth, freckled, pimply, blotchy

Mouth, lips, teeth: wide, thin, straight, pearly, stained, bad, decayed, gleaming, irregular, projecting, prominent, uneven, well-brushed, thick

Character: humble, kind-hearted, proud, haughty, vain, greedy, selfish, cheerful, miserable, gloomy, affectionate, honest, charming, spiteful, mean, loyal, generous, adorable, sincere, detestable, lovable, earnest, stubborn, obstinate, fanatical, enthusiastic, timid, bold, excitable, impetuous

Clothing: Think of the many different kinds of garments you have seen and make a list of them.

Habits: Make a list of these from your own observations of people, from characters in films or television shows and from characters in the books you read.

Voice: low, high-pitched, squeaky, sweet, shrill, hoarse, deep, harsh, grating, rasping, tenor, bass, agreeable, melodious, husky, raucous, sepulchral, nasal, guttural

EXERCISE 189

Having a plan of the work, together with the necessary tools, you are now able to make a start. Write descriptions of any of the following people:

1. An old sailor seated on an upturned boat at the seaside.
2. A gipsy woman who has called at your house.
3. Any boy or girl in your class.
4. An elderly clergyman seated in his study.
5. Any member of your own family.
6. A little boy who has just arrived at his friend's birthday party.
7. The postman who delivers the mail in your street.
8. A gardener who is taking a rest after a spell of hard digging.
9. A circus clown.
10. A butcher in whose shop several customers are waiting.
11. A soldier on sentry duty.
12. A stage or television comedian.
13. A bricklayer at work.
14. A conjurer who is giving an entertainment at school.
15. A nurse who is attending to the wants of her patients.
16. The conductor of a famous choir or orchestra.
17. A fussy old lady who is buying a new hat for Easter.
18. A man who is fishing from a river bank.
19. One of your neighbours. (See if your family can identify this person.)
20. A baby of about twelve months who is sitting in its pram.

Describing Rooms

Study these descriptions of rooms carefully. Notice how the writer has succeeded in giving his readers a clear picture of the room he has in mind.

Dotheboy's Hall

It was a bare and dirty room, with a couple of windows, whereof a tenth part might be glass, the remainder being stopped up with copybooks and paper. There were a couple of long, old rickety desks, cut and notched, and inked, and damaged in every possible way; two or three forms, a detached desk for Mr. Squeers, and another for his assistant. The ceiling was supported, like that of a barn, by cross beams and rafters; and the walls were so stained and discoloured that it was impossible to tell whether they had ever been touched with paint or whitewash.

(Nicholas Nickleby—Charles Dickens)

Fagin's Den

The walls and ceiling of the room were perfectly black with age and dirt. There was a deal table before the fire, upon which were a candle, stuck in a ginger-beer bottle, two or three pewter pots, a loaf and butter, and a plate. In a frying-pan which was on the fire, and which was secured to the mantelshelf by a string, some sausages were cooking; and standing over them, with a toasting-fork in his hand, was a very old shrivelled Jew, who seemed to be dividing his attention between the frying-pan and a clothes-horse, over which a great number of silk handkerchiefs were hanging. Several rough beds, made of old sacks, were huddled side by side on the floor; and seated round the table were four or five boys.

(Oliver Twist—Charles Dickens)

Peggotty's Home

The bedroom was the completest and most desirable ever seen—in the stern of the vessel; with a little window, where the rudder used to go through; a little looking-glass, just the right height for me nailed against the wall, and framed with oyster-shells; a little bed which there was just enough room to get into; and a nosegay of seaweed in a blue mug on the table. The walls were whitewashed as white as milk, and the patchwork counterpane made my eyes quite ache with its brightness.

(David Copperfield—Charles Dickens)

Describing Rooms

In writing a description of a room you should bear in mind the following points:

1. Shape and size. Is it round, oblong, square or irregular in shape? How long, high and wide is it?

2. How are the walls decorated? Are they painted, papered, distempered, whitewashed, colour-washed, etc.? Is there a frieze? Is there a dado? Is there oak panelling? What pictures, plaques, or other ornaments are there on the walls?

3. How many windows are there? What type and size are they? Are they sash windows, bay or bow, casement, french, latticed or dormer windows? Have they curtains or blinds, or both?

4. Is the ceiling plain or decorated? Are any rafters visible? Is the floor tiled, boarded, flagged, blocked or concreted?

5. How is the floor covered? Carpet with stained surround? Partly or completely covered with linoleum? Stained and uncovered except for rugs here and there?

6. What type of heating is used? Central heating with radiators? Coal fire? Gas fire? Electric fire or radiator? Anthracite stove?

7. How is it lighted at night? Gas? Electric light? Oil lamp, etc.?

8. Furniture? Oak, mahogany, walnut, deal, etc.? Type, size and shape of chairs, table, sideboard, cupboard, dresser, etc.

You spend about a thousand hours in your classroom during the year, so you should know quite a lot about it. Can you write a clear description of it, one which will enable a person reading it to form a realistic picture of it in his mind? Remember all the points mentioned when writing.

Describing Rooms

Write a clear description of one or more of the rooms named below.

1. A kitchen or kitchenette
2. A library
3. The vestry of a church
4. An artist's studio
5. The room of your headmaster or headmistress
6. A large office in which clerks and typists are at work
7. A butcher's shop
8. An attic bedroom
9. A lounge in a large house
10. A lumber room
11. A school canteen
12. A gymnasium
13. A waiting-room in a railway station
14. A hospital ward in which there are several patients
15. A small café or restaurant
16. The living-room of your house
17. The nicest room you have ever seen
18. The kind of room you would like for your very own
19. The interior of a modern caravan
20. Any room you have occupied in a guest-house

Comprehension 1

PIP SMOKES A PIPE

One fine day, as Pip was wandering through the wood, he saw a young man seated at the foot of a tree puffing at a pipe. At that sight Pip opened his eyes very wide and remained spellbound.

"Oh!" he said to himself, "if only I could have a pipe too! Oh, if only I could send those lovely clouds of smoke from my mouth! Oh, if only I could go home smoking like a chimney!"

While these wonderful ideas chased each other through the little monkey's mind, all of a sudden the young man, who was tired with the heat of the day, gave a couple of tremendous yawns and, laying down his pipe on the grass, promptly fell asleep.

What did that rogue of a Pip do then?

He approached the sleeper very quietly, stretched out one paw very gingerly, and, snatching the pipe from the grass, fled away with it like the wind.

As soon as he got home he called his father, mother and brothers, and taking the large pipe between his teeth, he began to smoke. When his mother and brothers saw clouds of smoke pouring from his mouth they laughed as if they had gone mad; but his father said to him, "Take care, Pip! If you go mimicking men like this you will turn into a man some day, and then. . . . Why, you will bitterly repent, but it will be too late!"

Struck by these words, Pip took the pipe out of his mouth and did not smoke it again.

(*The Story of Pip*—Carlo Collodi)

1. What did Pip see as he wandered through the wood one day?
2. What did this sight make Pip want to do?
3. What made the young man so tired?
4. What did the young man do after yawning?
5. What did Pip do after the young man dropped off to sleep?
6. Why did Pip's mother and brothers laugh as if they had gone mad?
7. What warning did Pip's father give him?
8. In what way did Pip show that he took notice of this warning?

Comprehension 2

THE OLD MAN OF THE SEA

After a time I saw a little old man making signs to me to carry him on my back over the brook. Having pity on his age I did so, but when I would have put him down on the other side he twisted his legs so tightly round my neck that I fell to the ground half choked.

Though he saw how faint I was, he made no sign of getting off, but, opening his legs a little to let me breathe better, he dug his feet into my stomach to make me rise and carry him further. Day after day, and night after night he clung to me, until by good luck I got rid of him in the following way.

Coming to a spot where, a few days before, I had left the juice of some grapes in a calabash, I drank the juice which, in the meantime, had become very good wine. This gave me fresh strength, and instead of dragging myself wearily along, I danced and sang with right good-will. The old man, seeing how lighthearted the wine had made me, signed to me to give him some. He took a deep drink and soon became so merry that he loosed his hold on my shoulders, when I tossed him off and killed him with a big stone, lest he should make me his victim once more.

Some sailors whom I met shortly afterwards said I was the first person they had known to escape from the old man of the sea, who for years had been a terror to those obliged to visit the island.

(Sinbad the Sailor—The Arabian Nights)

1. What did the old man want the writer to do?
2. Why did the writer have pity on the old man?
3. What did the old man do when the writer (Sinbad) wanted to put him down?
4. Why did the old man dig his feet into Sinbad's stomach?
5. What did the old man do to let Sinbad breathe more easily?
6. How had the wine in the calabash been made?
7. What effect did the wine have on Sinbad?
8. What did Sinbad do after drinking the wine?
9. What did Sinbad do after tossing the old man off his back?
10. What did the sailors tell Sinbad?

ALICE AND THE WHITE RABBIT

Alice was beginning to get very tired of sitting by her sister on the bank, and of having nothing to do; once or twice she had peeped into the book her sister was reading, but it had no pictures or conversations in it, "and what is the use of a book," thought Alice, "without pictures or conversations?"

So she was considering in her own mind (as well as she could, for the hot day made her feel very sleepy and stupid) whether the pleasure of making a daisy-chain would be worth the trouble of getting up and picking the daisies, when suddenly a White Rabbit with pink eyes ran close by her.

There was nothing so very remarkable in that; nor did Alice think it so very much out of the way to hear the Rabbit say to itself, "Oh dear! Oh dear! I shall be too late!" But when the Rabbit actually took a watch out of its waistcoat pocket, and looked at it, and then hurried on, Alice started to her feet, for it flashed across her mind that she had never before seen a rabbit with either a waistcoat-pocket, or a watch to take out of it, and, burning with curiosity, she ran across the field after it, and was just in time to see it pop down a large rabbit-hole under the hedge.

(*Alice in Wonderland*—Lewis Carroll)

1. Where was Alice sitting?
2. Who was with her?
3. What was this person doing?
4. Why was Alice not interested in this occupation?
5. What did Alice consider making?
6. Why did Alice feel very sleepy and stupid?
7. What was the colour of the White Rabbit's eyes?
8. What did the White Rabbit say to itself?
9. What did the White Rabbit take out of its waistcoat-pocket?
10. Where did the White Rabbit go to?

Comprehension 4

TOM AND THE POACHERS

It was a clear, still night, and the moon shone so brightly through the water that Tom could not sleep.

Suddenly, he saw a beautiful sight. A bright red light moved along the river-side, and threw down into the water a long flame. Tom, curious little rogue, must needs go and see what it was; so he swam to the shore, and met the light as it stopped over a shallow at the edge of a low rock. And there, underneath the light, lay five or six great salmon, looking up at the flame with their great goggle eyes, and wagging their tails, as if they were very much pleased at it.

Tom came to the top to look at this wonderful light nearer, and made a splash. And he heard a voice say: "There was a fish rose."

He did not know what the words meant: but he seemed to know the sound of them, and the voice which spoke them: and he saw on the bank three great two-legged creatures, one of whom held the light, and another a long pole.

Tom felt that there was danger coming, and longed to warn the foolish salmon, who kept staring up at the light. But before he could make up his mind, down came the pole through the water. There was a fearful splash and a struggle, and Tom saw that a poor salmon was speared right through, and was lifted out of the water.

(*The Water-Babies*—Charles Kingsley)

1. Why was Tom unable to sleep that night?
2. What was the beautiful sight that Tom saw?
3. What did Tom do when he saw it?
4. What did Tom see underneath the light?
5. Why did Tom rise to the surface of the water?
6. What did he hear when he reached the surface?
7. Who stood on the bank of the river?
8. What were they carrying?
9. What did Tom long to do?
10. What happened before he could make up his mind to do it?

THE BREAD-FRUIT TREE

Jack and I examined the bread-fruit tree. We were much struck with its broad leaves, which were twelve or eighteen inches long, deeply indented, and of a glossy smoothness, like the laurel.

The tree bears two or three crops of fruit in a year; very much like wheaten bread in appearance it is round in shape, about six inches in diameter, and it has a rough rind. It forms the principal food of many South Sea islanders. The fruit on the tree which we inspected hung in clusters of twos and threes on the branches, and were of various colours, from light pea-green to brown and rich yellow. Jack said that the yellow fruit was the ripe fruit.

The trunk was twenty feet high, being quite destitute of branches up to that height, where it branched off into a beautiful head. The wood, which is durable and of a good colour, is used to build native houses; the bark of the young branches being made into cloth.

Another product of this wonderful tree is gum, which serves the natives for pitching their canoes.

(The Coral Island—R. M. Ballantyne)

1. Write three common adjectives which describe a leaf of a bread-fruit tree.
2. What is the fruit like in appearance?
3. Why is the tree very important to the natives?
4. How does the fruit hang on the branches?
5. How could you recognize a ripe bread-fruit?
6. How many crops of fruit does the bread-fruit tree produce in a year?
7. How far above the ground was the lowest branch of the tree which the boys were looking at?
8. Which part of the tree is used by the natives for making cloth?
9. What is meant by 'pitching their canoes'?
0. Write the word in this extract which means 'hard-wearing'.

Comprehension 6

TAMING A WILD HORSE

Dick went up boldly to the wild horse and patted its head and stroked its nose, for nothing is so likely to alarm either a tame or a wild horse as any appearance of timidity or hesitation on the part of those who approach them. Then he stroked its neck and shoulders —the horse eyeing him nervously all the time.

This done, Dick went down to the stream, filled his cap with water, and carried it to the horse, which sniffed suspiciously and backed a little; so he laid the cap down and went and patted him again. Presently he took up the cap and carried it to the animal's nose. The poor creature was almost choking with thirst, so that the moment he understood what was in the cap, he buried his lips in it and sucked it up.

Dick filled his cap three times, the horse drinking until its burning thirst was quenched, then Dick went up to his shoulder, patted him, undid the line that fastened him, and vaulted lightly on his back. At this unexpected act the horse plunged and reared a great deal, but Dick stroked him until he became quiet again, and having done so urged him into a gallop over the plains. By degrees they broke into a furious gallop, and after breathing him well, Dick returned and tied him to the tree. Then he rubbed him down and gave him another drink. This time the horse smelt his new master all over, and Dick felt that he had conquered him by kindness.

(The Dog Crusoe—R. M. Ballantyne)

1. What did Dick do after going boldly up to the wild horse?
2. What is most likely to alarm a horse when someone approaches?
3. What did the horse do when Dick stroked its neck and shoulders?
4. In what did Dick carry the water he fetched for the horse?
5. What did the horse do the first time Dick offered him a drink?
6. What did the horse do when he understood what was in Dick's cap?
7. What did Dick do after the horse had quenched its thirst?
8. What effect did this have on the horse?
9. What did Dick do after quietening the horse by stroking him?
10. What did the horse do after Dick had rubbed him down and given him another drink?

THE ISLE OF PALMS

On reaching the Isle of Palms the pirates at once proceeded to take in those stores of which they stood in need. The harbour into which the schooner ran was a narrow bay, on the shores of which the palm trees grew sufficiently high to prevent her masts being seen from the other side of the island. Here the captives were landed, but as Manton did not wish them to witness his proceedings he sent them across the islet under the escort of a party which conveyed them to the shores of a small bay. On the rocks in this bay lay the wreck of what had once been a noble ship. It was now completely dismantled.

On a green knoll near the margin of this bay a rude tent or hut was constructed by the pirates out of part of an old sail which had been washed ashore, and some broken spars. A small cask of biscuit and two or three blankets were placed in it, and here the captives were left to do as they pleased until such time as Manton chose to send for them. The only piece of advice that was given to them by their surly jailer was that they should not on any pretence whatever cross the island to the bay in which the schooner lay at anchor.

(*Gascoyne*—R. M. Ballantyne)

1. What did the pirates do on reaching the Isle of Palms?
2. In what kind of ship did they travel?
3. What kind of trees grew on the shores of the harbour?
4. Why were the ship's masts not visible from the other side of the island?
5. Why did Manton send the captives to the bay on the other side of the island?
6. What lay on the rocks in this bay?
7. What did the pirates construct on the green knoll near the edge of this bay?
8. Name the two things which were used in constructing it.
9. What food did the pirates leave for their captives?
10. What did the surly jailer warn the captives not to do?

Comprehension 8

LION COUNTRY

Mr. Rogers and his party trekked on for some miles that evening, and soon after sundown halted by the side of a wood, whose edges were composed of dense thorns, and here, at the General's suggestion, all set to work, after the waggon had been drawn up in a suitable position, to cut down the bushes so as to make a square patch, with the dense thorns on three sides and the waggon on the fourth, the lower part of the waggon being fortified with the bushes that were cut down.

The object was to form a sound enclosure, which was duly strengthened, so as to protect the horses and bullocks from the wild beasts that haunted the neighbourhood.

It was very hard work, and Dinny grumbled terribly, till Dick said quietly to his brother, in Dinny's hearing: "I wonder that Dinny doesn't work harder. The General says this part swarms with lions; and they'll be down upon us before we've done if he doesn't make haste."

Dinny seemed for the moment to be turned into stone, at the bare mention of the word 'lions'; but directly afterwards he was toiling away with feverish haste, and in quite a state of excitement, bullying Coffee and Chicory for not bringing in more dead wood for the fire.

(*Off to the Wilds*—George Manville Fenn)
(By kind permission of Messrs. Sampson Low, Ltd.)

1. At what time of day did Mr. Rogers' party halt?
2. Where did they halt?
3. What were the edges of this place composed of?
4. What formed three of the sides of the square patch which they made?
5. What formed the fourth side of this square patch?
6. Why was this enclosure made?
7. To what use did the party put the bushes they cut down?
8. Who suggested making this enclosure?
9. What word had the effect of making Dinny appear 'turned into stone'?
10. What did Dinny do after recovering a little from his fright?

MR. CREAKLE

In the dormitory that evening we had a secret banquet, bought with my money; and I (David Copperfield) heard all kinds of things about the school and all belonging to it. I heard that Mr. Creakle was the sternest of masters; that he laid about him, right and left, every day of his life, slashing away unmercifully. That he knew nothing himself except the art of slashing, being more ignorant than the lowest boy in the school; that he had been, a good many years ago, a small hop-dealer in London.

I heard that the man with the wooden leg, whose name was Tungay, had formerly assisted in the hop business, but had come to the school with Mr. Creakle because he had broken his leg in Mr. Creakle's service. I heard that, with the exception of Mr. Creakle, Tungay considered the whole establishment, masters and boys, as his natural enemies, and that the only delight of his life was to be sour and malicious.

But the greatest wonder that I heard of Mr. Creakle was that he never ventured to lay a hand on one boy in the school, and that was J. Steerforth.

The hearing of this, and a good deal more, outlasted the banquet some time. The greater part of the guests had gone to bed as soon as the eating and drinking were over; and we, who had remained whispering and listening half undressed, at last went off to bed, too.

(*David Copperfield*—Charles Dickens)

1. Where was the banquet held?
2. Who paid for it?
3. What did Mr. Creakle do to his pupils every day of his life?
4. What had Mr. Creakle been before he took up teaching?
5. Why had Mr. Creakle brought his assistant Mr. Tungay into the teaching profession with him?
6. How did Mr. Tungay regard the masters and pupils of the school?
7. Which boy was never punished by Mr. Creakle?
8. What did most of the guests do when the eating and drinking were over?
9. What did the rest of the party do?
0. What was Mr. Tungay's only delight in life?

Comprehension 10

MUSKRAT CASTLE

Muskrat Castle, as the house had been humorously named by some waggish officer, stood in an open lake, fully a quarter of a mile distant from the nearest shore. On every side the water extended much further, the precise position being about two miles from the northern end of the lake and nearly a mile from the eastern shore. As there was not the smallest appearance of an island, but the house stood on piles, with the water flowing beneath it, and Deerslayer had already discovered that the lake was of great depth, he asked for an explanation of this strange circumstance. Hurry solved the puzzle by telling him that on the spot where the house stood, a long, narrow shoal, which extended a few hundred yards in a north and south direction, rose to within six or eight feet of the surface of the lake, and that Tom Hutter had driven piles into it and built his house on them for the purpose of security.

"The old fellow was burnt out three times between the Indians and the hunters," explained Hurry, "and in one fight with the redskins he lost his only son, since which time he has taken to the water for safety. No one can attack him here without coming in a boat, and old Tom is well supplied with arms and ammunition, and the castle, as you may see, is a tight breastwork against light shot."

(*The Deerslayer*—J. Fenimore Cooper)

1. Who had given Muskrat Castle its name?
2. How far was it from the nearest shore of the lake?
3. Which was the nearer to Muskrat Castle, the northern shore of the lake or the eastern shore?
4. How was the house supported?
5. About how deep was the water immediately beneath the house?
6. In which direction did the shoal run?
7. How long was this shoal?
8. Why had Hutter built his house where it was?
9. How many sons did Hutter have when he went to live in Muskrat Castle.
10. How was Hutter equipped to defend his house against enemy attacks?

SAVED FROM THE CRUEL SEA

At this moment the windows of the cottage shook violently at the loud report of a cannon that appeared almost close to the cliff. All sprang to their feet, and looking through the window saw rocket after rocket whizzing high in the air. As Paul and Ned rushed out to the terrace a fearful sight was presented. Brightly illumined by a blue light the revenue cutter lay fixed on the Iron Rock. A wave rolled completely over her, and at once extinguished the light; at the same moment a tremendous crash was heard as her mast fell over the side.

Without loss of time Paul and Ned had seized two coils of rope from the cottage stores, and were making their way along the cliff to the projecting point at the right of the entrance to the bay.

Before long the mast, with six men clinging to it, was washed against the cliff exactly below the Point. But by the time Paul and Ned arrived only one remained alive—a negro of about fourteen, whom they rescued by means of ropes.

The three now cautiously picked their way among the loose stones on the dangerous paths, and soon arrived at the cottage, where the negro boy was made comfortable and fed, and was soon fast asleep upon some clean straw in the kitchen.

(Cast Up By The Sea—Sir S. W. Baker)

1. What caused the windows of the cottage to shake?
2. Where did the noise appear to come from?
3. What did the occupants of the cottage see when they looked through the window?
4. What did Paul and Ned see on the Iron Rock?
5. How was the blue light which had illumined the vessel extinguished?
6. What caused the tremendous crash which Paul and Ned heard at that instant?
7. How many men were clinging to the mast of the wrecked vessel?
8. What did Paul and Ned take with them when they made their way along the cliff?
9. Who was the only survivor after the mast had been washed against the cliff?
10. Where did this survivor sleep after his rescue?

Comprehension 12

THE BELL ROCK COLLECTION

There was a grand procession through the streets of the two towns of Perth and Dundee. The holy abbots, in their robes, walked under gilded canopies; the monks chanted; flags and banners were carried by seamen, and lighted tapers by penitents. St. Antonio, the patron of those who trust to the stormy ocean, was carried in all pomp through the streets; and as the procession passed, coins of various value were thrown down by those who watched it from the windows, and, as fast as thrown, were collected by little boys dressed as angels.

Everyone gave freely, for there were few, indeed none, who, if not in their own circle, at least among their acquaintances, had not to deplore the loss of someone dear to them, or to those they visited, from the dangerous rock which lay in the very track of all vessels entering the Firth of Tay.

These processions had been arranged in order that a sufficient sum of money might be collected to enable them to put into execution a plan, which had been proposed by an adventurous young seaman at a meeting specially called for the purpose, of fixing a bell on the rock, which could be so arranged that the slightest breath of wind would cause the hammer of it to sound, and thus, by its tolling, warn the mariner of his danger; and the sums given were more than sufficient.

(*The Legend of the Bell Rock*—Captain Marryat)

1. Why was the procession held?
2. Name the two towns in which it was held.
3. Who chanted in the procession?
4. Who carried the flags and banners?
5. What is the name of the patron saint of sailors?
6. Who collected the coins which were thrown down by the people watching from the windows?
7. How were the collectors dressed?
8. Who had proposed fixing a bell to the dangerous rock?
9. Why did everybody give so generously?
10. Why was this rock so dangerous?

THE CHILDREN'S OCCUPATIONS

As soon as the children were dressed Jacob said:

"My dear children, you know that you must stay in this cottage so that the wicked troopers may not find you; they killed your father, and if I had not taken you away they would have burnt you in your beds. You must therefore live here as my children, and you must call yourselves by the name of Armitage, and not that of Beverley; and you must do everything for yourselves, for you can have no servants to wait upon you. Edward is the oldest so he must go out with me in the forest, and I must teach him to kill deer and other game for food."

"And Humphrey," went on Jacob, "you must look after the pony and the pigs, and dig in the garden with Edward and me when we are not hunting, and you and Alice must light the fire and clean the house in the morning. Then you, Humphrey, will go to the spring for water, for Alice to do the washing; then you will help her to make the dinner and make the beds. And little Edith shall take care of the fowls, and feed them every morning, and collect the eggs they lay."

(*The Children of the New Forest*—Captain Marryat)

1. Why did the children have to remain in the cottage?
2. What had happened to the children's father?
3. What would probably have happened to the children if Jacob had not taken them away from their home?
4. What was the real surname of the children?
5. What surname did Jacob tell them to use during their stay at the cottage?
6. Which of the children had to go hunting with Jacob, and why was he chosen?
7. Which animals did Humphrey have to look after?
8. Give the names of the three persons who had to dig in the garden when there was no hunting.
9. From where did Humphrey fetch water?
0. Which of the children had to feed the fowls and collect the eggs?

Comprehension 14

THE DESTRUCTION OF POMPEII

At that moment they felt the earth shake beneath their feet; the walls of the theatre trembled, and in the distance they heard the crash of falling roofs. An instant more and the mountain-cloud seemed to roll towards them, dark and rapid, like a torrent; at the same time it cast forth from its bosom a shower of ashes mixed with vast fragments of burning stone. Over the crushing vines—over the desolate streets—over the amphitheatre itself—far and wide—with many a mighty splash in the agitated sea fell that awful shower.

No longer thought the crowd of justice; safety for themselves was now their sole thought. Each turned to fly—each dashing, pressing, crushing against the other. Trampling recklessly over the fallen amidst groans, and oaths, and prayers, and sudden shrieks—the enormous crowd vomited itself forth through the numerous passages. Some, anticipating a second earthquake, hastened to their homes to load themselves with their more costly goods, and escape while there was yet time; others, dreading the showers of ashes which now fell fast, torrent upon torrent, over the streets, rushed under the roofs of the nearest houses, or temples, or sheds—shelter of any kind—for protection from the terrors of the open air.

(*The Last Days of Pompeii*—Lord Lytton)

1. What did the people hear in the distance?
2. What did the mountain-cloud seem to do?
3. What came out of this mountain-cloud?
4. What fell with a mighty splash into the agitated sea?
5. What was the sole thought of the crowd as they fled?
6. What did some people think would happen?
7. Why did these people hasten to their homes?
8. Why did others rush under the roofs of the nearest buildings?
9. Was the town of Pompeii an inland town or a coastal town? Give a reason for your answer.
10. Name four kinds of sounds which escaped from the lips of the fugitives.

BUILDING AN IGLOO

First of all the Eskimo drew out a long knife, with the point of which he drew a circle of about seven feet in diameter. Two feet to one side of this circle he drew a smaller one, of about four feet in diameter. Next, he cut out of the snow a number of hard blocks, which he arranged round the large circle, building them above each other in such a manner that they gradually rose in the form of a dome. The chinks between them he filled compactly with soft snow, and the last block introduced into the top of the structure was formed exactly on the principle of the keystone of an arch. When the large dome was finished he commenced the smaller; and in the course of two hours both the houses—or igloos, as the Eskimos call them—were completed.

Two holes were left in them to serve as doors; and after they were finished the Eskimo cut a square hole in the top of each, not far from the keystones and above the entrances. Into these he fitted slabs of clear ice, which formed windows as beautiful and useful as if they had been made of glass. There were two doorways in the large igloo, one of which faced the doorway of the smaller. Between these he built an arched passage, so that the two were thus connected, and the small hut formed a sort of inner chamber to the larger.

(*Ungava*—R. M. Ballantyne)

1. What did the Eskimo use for drawing the circles?
2. What was the diameter of the larger circle, and also of the smaller one?
3. How far away from the larger circle was the smaller one?
4. In what shape were the blocks of snow arranged?
5. What was used to fill in the chinks between the blocks of snow?
6. What purpose did the last block of snow fulfil?
7. Which of the two igloos was finished first?
8. How many doors were there in the larger igloo?
9. What were the windows of the igloo made of?
10. How were the two igloos connected?

Comprehension 16

EXPLORING AFRICA

Just before dark I took up my lodging for the night at a small village, where I procured some victuals for myself, and some corn for my horse, at the moderate price of a button, and was told that I should see the River Niger early next day.

The lions here are very numerous; the gates are shut a little after sunset, and nobody allowed to go out. The thought of seeing the Niger in the morning, and the troublesome buzzing of mosquitoes, prevented me from shutting my eyes during the night; and I had saddled my horse and was in readiness before daylight; but on account of the wild beasts I was obliged to wait until the people were stirring, and the gates opened. This happened to be a market-day at Sego, and the roads were everywhere filled with people carrying different articles to sell. I passed four large villages, and at eight o'clock saw the smoke over Sego.

As I approached the town, I saw with infinite pleasure the object of my mission—the long-sought-for majestic Niger, glittering in the morning sun and flowing slowly to the eastward. I hastened to the brink, and, having drunk of the water, I lifted up my fervent thanks in prayer to the Great Ruler of all things.

(*Travels in Africa*—Mungo Park)

1. Where did the writer take up his lodging for the night?
2. What did he give his horse to eat?
3. What was he told he would see early the next day?
4. What animals were numerous near the place where the writer lodged?
5. At what time of day were the gates of the village shut?
6. Name two things which prevented the writer from sleeping that night.
7. When was the writer ready to continue his journey?
8. Why did he have to delay his departure?
9. What did the people who thronged the roads carry?
10. What did the writer do when he saw the river?

IN A HINDU TEMPLE

Passepartout, having purchased the articles for his master, took a ride through the city of Bombay, but unfortunately his curiosity led him further than it was wise to go. It happend to be the day of one of the Parsee festivals, and after wandering about for some time he turned his steps towards a pretty hill-suburb.

As he neared the wonderful pagoda on Malabar Hill it occurred to him he would like to see the interior. On two points he was quite ignorant; first, that there are certain Hindu temples which Christians are not permitted to enter; and secondly, that even Hindus are not allowed entrance without first leaving their shoes at the door.

Passepartout went in like a simple tourist, and was soon lost in admiration of the gorgeous ornamentation which everywhere met his eyes. Suddenly he found himself sprawling on the floor of the sacred building, for three priests, with fury in their looks, rushed upon him, tore off his shoes and stockings, and began to beat him. But the agile Frenchman was soon on his feet again, and lost no time in knocking down two of his adversaries with a couple of well-directed blows; then, rushing out of the pagoda as fast as his legs could carry him, he soon outdistanced the third priest, who had followed him, and mingling with the crowd in the streets he thus escaped.

(Round the World in Eighty Days—Jules Verne)

1. What did Passepartout do after making his purchases?
2. What was being held in the city that day?
3. What did Passepartout want to do when he got near the pagoda?
4. What are people expected to do before entering a Hindu temple?
5. Why was Passepartout lost in admiration after entering the temple?
6. Who attacked Passepartout as he was looking round?
7. What did they do to his shoes and stockings?
8. What did Passepartout do immediately after getting to his feet again?
9. How many priests pursued Passepartout?
0. How did he manage to escape?

Comprehension 18

THE LEPER

The grey light of early morning showed them a footpath wandering among the gorse, upon which stood a white figure. It paused a little and seemed to look about; and then, at a slow pace, and bent almost double, it began to draw near across the heath. At every step the bell clanked. Face it had none; a white hood, not even pierced with eye-holes, veiled the head; and as the creature moved it seemed to feel its way with the tapping of a stick. Fear fell upon the lads, as cold as death.

"A leper!" said Dick hoarsely.

"His touch is death," said Matcham. "Let us run."

"Not so," returned Dick. "See! He is stone-blind. He guides himself with a staff. Let us lie still; the wind blows towards the path, and he will go by and not hurt us."

The blind leper was now about half-way towards them, and just then the sun rose and shone full on his veiled face. The dismal beating of the bell which he carried, the pattering of the stick, and the eyeless screen before his countenance filled the lads with dismay; and at every step that brought him nearer their strength and courage seemed to desert them. At last he came level with the pit, where he paused and turned his face full upon the lads for some seconds; then he began to move on again, and after crossing the remainder of the little heath disappeared into the woods.

(*The Black Arrow*—Robert Louis Stevenson)

1. At what time of day did this incident take place?
2. What grew on either side of the footpath?
3. What covered the head of the leper?
4. Why was this covering not even pierced with eye-holes?
5. How did the leper give warning of his approach?
6. How did he feel his way along the path?
7. Why did Matcham want to run away?
8. Why did Dick consider this unnecessary?
9. What did the leper do as he drew level with the pit?
10. Where did the leper go after crossing the little heath?

CROSSING THE ANDES

As we set out for the Portillo Pass our manner of travelling was delightfully independent. In the inhabited parts we bought a little firewood, hired pasture for the animals, and bivouacked in the corner of the same field with them. Carrying an iron pot, we cooked and ate our supper under a cloudless sky, and knew no trouble. My companions were Mariano Gonzales, who had formerly accompanied me in Chile, and a muleteer with his ten mules and a 'madrina'.

The madrina (or godmother) is an old steady mare with a bell round her neck; and wherever she goes the mules follow her. The affection of these animals for their madrinas saves much trouble. If several large troops are turned into one field to graze, in the morning the muleteers have only to lead the madrinas a little apart and tinkle their bells; and although there may be two or three hundred together, each mule immediately knows the bell of its own madrina and comes to her. It is nearly impossible to lose an old mule; for if it is detained for several hours by force, she will, by the power of smell, track out the madrina.

Of our ten animals six were for riding and four for carrying cargoes, each taking turn about. We carried a good deal of food in case we should be snowed up, as the season was rather late for crossing the Andes.

(*The Voyage of the Beagle*—Charles Darwin)

1. Which of the writer's companions had travelled with him before?
2. Why did the party carry a good deal of food?
3. In what did the party cook their food?
4. Name three things which the party did in the inhabited parts of the country.
5. Write the phrase which shows that the weather was fine.
6. What is a madrina?
7. Why is a madrina so useful?
8. Why is it almost impossible for a muleteer to lose an old mule?
9. How many of the mules were needed to carry the food?
0. How many were used for riding?

Comprehension 20

ATTACKED BY ROBBERS

My father, John Ridd, had been killed by the Doones of Bag worthy while riding home from Porlock market with six other farmers one Saturday evening. These robbers had no grudge against him, for he never flouted them because they robbed other people. The seven were jogging along when suddenly a horseman stopped in the starlight full across them, and though he seemed one man against seven it was really one man against one, for of the six who were with him there was not one who did not pull out his money.

But father set his staff about his head and rode at the Doone robber, who avoided the sudden attack. Then, when Smiler was carried away by the dash and weight of my father, the outlaw plundered the rest of the party. As father returned to help them he found himself in the midst of a dozen men, who seemed to come out of a turf-rick, some on horse, some on foot. He smote lustily with his staff, cracking three or four crowns, until the rest drew their horses away, and he thought he was master. But a man beyond the range of his staff was crouching by the peat-stack with a long gun set to his shoulder, and he got poor father against the sky. Smiler came home with blood upon him, and father was found in the morning dead upon the moor, with his cudgel lying broken under him.

(*Lorna Doone*—R. D. Blackmore)

1. Where was John Ridd returning from when he was killed?
2. Who were riding with him?
3. Why did the Doones have no grudge against John Ridd?
4. What did John Ridd's companions do when they were stopped by the robber?
5. What did John Ridd do then?
6. What was the name of John Ridd's horse?
7. How many robbers did John see when he returned to help his companions?
8. Were all these robbers on horseback?
9. What did the robbers do after John Ridd had cracked the crowns of three or four of them?
10. Where was the robber who shot John Ridd?

ANSWERS

Exercise 2

1. boy; football
2. woman; dog; bone
3. cat; hand
4. orange; apple; banana
5. monkey; nuts; children
6. fireman; ladder; child
7. teacher; class; boomerang
8. kitten; ball; wool
9. eagle; beak; talons
10. robin; bird; breast

Exercise 4

1. saddle
2. stag
3. shamrock
4. spawn
5. sandal
6. shoal
7. sculptor
8. scuttle
9. skeleton
10. swine

Exercise 5

1. cherries
2. gipsies
3. pansies
4. butterflies
5. flies
6. fairies
7. lorries
8. poppies

Exercise 6

1. berries
2. ponies
3. butterflies
4. ladies
5. injuries
6. diaries
7. lorries
8. stories
9. cities
10. hobbies

Exercise 7

1. loaves
2. knives
3. wolves
4. leaves
5. thieves
6. sheaves
7. shelves
8. wives
9. calves
10. halves

Exercise 9

1. boys; entries; diaries
2. foxes; bushes
3. bakers; loaves; shelves
4. sons-in-law
5. thieves
6. thieves
7. solos
8. valleys
9. builders; roofs
10. buffaloes; lions
11. peasants; sheaves
12. urchins; alleys
13. ladies; pianos
14. atlases
15. policemen; mysteries
16. torpedoes; ships
17. geese; turkeys
18. children; vases
19. mice
20. women; babies

Exercise 10

1. three knives
2. several chimneys
3. many pulleys
4. two halves
5. a pair of crutches
6. a bunch of pansies
7. a flock of sheep
8. two feet
9. a family of wolves
10. five donkeys

Exercise 11

1. suite
2. flight
3. fleet
4. set
5. bouquet (bunch)
6. packet
7. pack
8. library
9. batch
10. bundle

Exercise 12

1. bunch
2. box
3. suit
4. clump (forest)
5. sheaf
6. chest
7. string
8. bundle
9. collection
10. cluster
11. flock
12. herd
13. host
14. pack
15. shoal
16. school
17. swarm (hive)
18. troop
19. gang
20. litter

Exercise 13

1. flock
2. litter
3. clump
4. bunch
5. sheaf
6. set
7. flight
8. pack
9. suite
10. suit

Exercise 14

1. vegetables
2. tools
3. ships (vessels)
4. seasons
5. meats
6. liquids
7. musical instruments
8. continents
9. diseases
10. coins

Exercise 15

1. —— poultry
2. —— buildings
3. —— dogs
4. —— cereals
5. —— groceries
6. —— colours
7. —— countries
8. —— crockery
9. —— fruits
10. —— flowers

Exercise 16	Exercise 17	Exercise 18
1. corporal	1. cousin	1. bird
2. copra	2. sapphire	2. fruit
3. optimist	3. skirt	3. fish
4. chess	4. beech	4. tree
5. plough	5. gnat	5. vegetable
6. saw	6. sandals	6. metal
7. stone	7. draper	7. meat
8. cheque	8. wren	8. season
9. slippers	9. mackerel	9. tool
10. violet	10. wardrobe	10. colour

Exercise 19

1. reptiles
2. cutlery
3. occupations
4. insects
5. jewellery
6. stationery
7. vehicles
8. containers (bags)
9. kitchen utensils
10. hobbies

Exercise 20

1. niece (F)	11. lawn (N)
2. husband (M)	12. princess (F)
3. spade (N)	13. traveller (C)
4. scholar (C)	14. hotel (N)
5. nephew (M)	15. mistress (F)
6. bull (M)	16. monk (M)
7. guest (C)	17. secretary (C)
8. nun (F)	18. motor-car (N)
9. bride (F)	19. friend (C)
10. film (N)	20. host (M)

Exercise 21

1. prince	11. orphan
2. hero	12. guest (visitor)
3. bachelor	13. author
4. widower	14. patient
5. waiter	15. hearth
6. bride	16. anvil
7. fairy (witch)	17. camera
8. heiress	18. racket
9. matron	19. island
10. spinster	

Exercise 22

1. prince
2. gander
3. grandfather
4. bull
5. bridegroom
6. landlord
7. bucks
8. waiter
9. drake
10. stallion

Exercise 23

1. tigress
2. filly
3. sow
4. headmistress
5. queen
6. proprietress
7. niece
8. negress
9. ewes
10. heiress

Exercise 24

1. Duchess
2. Madam
3. rams
4. vixen
5. aunt
6. gentlemen
7. daughters
8. husband
9. hind
10. bitch

Exercise 25

1. waistcoat
2. blackboard
3. lighthouse
4. toothbrush
5. windmill
6. mousetrap
7. inkwell
8. eggcup
9. handbag
10. wheelbarrow

Exercise 26

1. workshop
2. milkman
3. watchmaker
4. ashtray
5. tablecloth
6. coalhouse
7. shopkeeper
8. headlines
9. bookshelf
10. crossroads

Exercise 27

I	II
1. homework	1. handcuff
2. shoelace	2. waterproof
3. bookmark	3. steamship
4. backbone	4. buttercup
5. keyhole	5. moonlight
6. bluebell	6. silkworm
7. hedgehog	7. sideboard
8. armchair	8. playground
9. strawberry	9. oatcake
10. pigsty	10. lumberjack

Exercise 28

1. football
2. footman
3. footpath
4. footprints
5. footstool
6. footwear
7. footwork
8. footsteps
9. footlights
10. footbridge

Exercise 29

1. clown's	11. cousin's
2. father's	12. friend's
3. dog's	13. robin's
4. workman's	14. doll's
5. month's	15. tortoise's
6. teacher's	16. tiger's
7. parent's	17. matron's
8. conductor's	18. nurse's
9. monkey's	19. Richard's
10. captain's	20. soldier's

Exercise 30

1. the cat's claws
2. the cow's horns
3. the clown's antics
4. the deer's antlers
5. the cobra's fangs
6. the donkey's ears
7. the pelican's beak
8. the fairy's wings
9. the blackbird's nest
10. Her Majesty's Ship

Exercise 31

1. parents'
2. men's
3. boys'
4. sailors'
5. miners'
6. ladies'
7. women's
8. birds'
9. eagles'
10. cooks'
11. children's
12. foxes'
13. babies'
14. kittens'
15. wolves'
16. teachers'
17. firemen's
18. dogs'
19. workmen's
20. charwomen's

Exercise 32

1. a boys' club
2. a ladies' cloakroom
3. a teachers' meeting
4. a workers' canteen
5. a children's paddling pool
6. men's overcoats
7. the girls' classroom
8. firemen's helmets
9. policemen's whistles
10. the Women's League

Exercise 33

1. cyclist's
2. teachers'
3. mouse's
4. baby's
5. policeman's
6. pupil's
7. babies'
8. pupils'
9. country's
10. cousins'

Exercise 34

1. dog's
2. father's
3. Despair's
4. Alice's
5. monkey's
6. Henry's; firemen's
7. people's
8. rabbits'
9. cat's
10. Fagin's
11. referee's; players'
12. girls'
13. (none)
14. (none)
15. horses'
16. rooks'
17. (none)
18. matron's
19. wasps'
20. (none)

Exercise 35

1. laughter
2. marriage
3. admiration
4. argument
5. ascent
6. behaviour
7. rebellion
8. trial
9. appearance
10. receipt

Exercise 36

1. allowance
2. explanation
3. defence
4. applause
5. comparison
6. declaration
7. permission
8. resemblance
9. subscription
10. occurrence

Exercise 37

1. performance
2. explosion
3. disturbance
4. arrival
5. intention
6. defiance
7. division
8. judgment
9. action
10. inquiry
11. movement
12. departure
13. satisfaction
14. proof
15. invitation
16. decision
17. hatred
18. growth
19. invasion
20. invention

Exercise 38

1. invaded
2. eat
3. sings
4. put
5. snapped
6. discovered
7. rode
8. washed; wiped
9. took; handed
10. likes; enjoys

Exercise 40

1. floats
2. purrs
3. dissolve
4. skate
5. scored
6. prosecuted
7. fined
8. sailed
9. discovered
10. prohibited

Exercise 41

1. inherit
2. broadcast
3. celebrate
4. disclose
5. denounce
6. solve
7. cancel
8. surmount
9. control
10. applaud

Exercise 42

1. saluted
2. quenched
3. committed
4. denied
5. awarded
6. skidded
7. accepted
8. demolished
9. performed
10. addressed

Exercise 43

1. shiver
2. flatter
3. scatter
4. postpone
5. revolve
6. squint
7. imitate
8. nibble
9. confess
10. vanish

Exercise 44

1. described
2. received
3. enclosed
4. encouraged
5. continued
6. explored
7. captured
8. refused
9. perspired
10. wasted

Exercise 45

1. hurried
2. supplied
3. occupied
4. copied
5. denied
6. satisfied
7. buried
8. studied
9. applied
10. replied

Exercise 46

1. knitted
2. stopped
3. pinned
4. skidded
5. travelled
6. occurred
7. dripped
8. stirred
9. compelled
10. preferred

Exercise 47

1. rang
2. spoke
3. rode
4. wrung
5. chose
6. drew
7. froze
8. did
9. sprang
10. taught
11. ate
12. burst
13. hurt
14. beat
15. rose
16. brought
17. saw
18. bore
19. fled
20. slew

Exercise 48

On the day of the picnic I **rose** early, **chose** a shirt with an open neck, **brought** it downstairs and **began** getting ready. During breakfast I **bit** my tongue and **hurt** it, so I **caught** hold of a mug of hot milk and **drank** some, but the mug **fell** to the floor and **broke.**

Exercise 49

1. sits; begins
2. tells; keeps
3. grow; learn
4. feels; goes
5. tears; writes
6. strikes; runs
7. sinks; sleeps
8. knows; is; gives
9. sells; pays
10. creeps; lies

Exercise 50

1. woke
2. dug
3. bent
4. bought
5. beat
6. flew
7. met
8. bled
9. was
10. came
11. hid
12. left
13. swam
14. sang
15. said
16. blew
17. tore
18. became
19. built
20. drove

Exercise 51

1. shouted
2. mutinied
3. admired
4. attracted
5. shovelled
6. trapped
7. remarked
8. produced
9. protected
10. prophesied
11. buried
12. permitted
13. controlled
14. noticed
15. cancelled
16. knitted
17. tidied
18. pursued
19. quarrelled
20. dropped

Exercise 52

1. wound
2. wrote
3. struck
4. gave
5. felt
6. held
7. thought
8. grew
9. fought
10. sank

Exercise 53

1. cut
2. drank
3. forgot
4. threw
5. took
6. broadcast
7. stole
8. dealt
9. leaped(leapt)
10. shook
11. wore
12. trod
13. dreaded
14. drowned
15. swore
16. found
17. forsook
18. dreamed (dreamt)
19. kneeled (knelt)
20. smelled (smelt)

Exercise 54

1. beaten
2. begun
3. eaten
4. done
5. broken
6. forgotten
7. frozen
8. chosen
9. drunk
10. stolen
11. worn
12. rung
13. drawn
14. spoken
15. bitten
16. flown
17. written
18. hidden
19. fallen
20. shaken

Exercise 55

1. Those lovely roses were grown by Father.
2. The leader of the gang was known to the police.
3. The winning car was driven by Stirling Moss.
4. The football was blown up by Robert.
5. The new carpet was laid by two men.
6. Several choruses were sung by the choir.
7. The lawns were mown by the gardener.
8. Gerald's coat was torn by barbed wire.
9. The dragon was slain by St. George.
10. The escaped convict was seen by a soldier.

Exercise 56

1. taken
2. given
3. thrown
4. trodden
5. swum
6. sewn
7. wound
8. run
9. held
10. caught
11. sworn
12. forsaken
13. sprung
14. shown
15. drowned
16. burst
17. borne
18. sunk
19. woven
20. hung

Exercise 57

1. sunny; cold
2. large; thrilling
3. hungry; angry
4. old; proud; new
5. ancient; skinny
6. Fine; fine
7. first; brilliant
8. black; shaggy
9. rough; woollen
10. tired; disheartened

Exercise 59

1. prosperous business
2. loyal subjects
3. celebrated pianist
4. rusty railings
5. muddy lane
6. fragrant flower
7. delicious pastries
8. fleecy clouds
9. changeable weather
10. severe injuries

Exercise 60

1. thinnest
2. oldest
3. most comfortable
4. worse
5. worst
6. more generous
7. most famous
8. most polite
9. fatter
10. better
11. most brilliant
12. heavier
13. most graceful
14. more difficult
15. most original
16. prettier
17. crudest
18. more powerful
19. sweetest
20. narrower

Exercise 62

Positive Degree	Comparative Degree	Superlative Degree
1. clever	cleverer	cleverest
2. rude	ruder	rudest
3. noisy	noisier	noisiest
4. jealous	more jealous	most jealous
5. patient	more patient	most patient
6. wealthy	wealthier	wealthiest
7. little	less	least
8. gracious	more gracious	most gracious
9. industrious	more industrious	most industrious
10. good	better	best
11. wide	wider	widest
12. cold	colder	coldest
13. bad	worse	worst
14. sturdy	sturdier	sturdiest
15. splendid	more splendid	most splendid
16. dirty	dirtier	dirtiest
17. faithful	more faithful	most faithful
18. ignorant	more ignorant	most ignorant
19. thin	thinner	thinnest
20. plucky	pluckier	pluckiest

Exercise 63

1. central
2. luxurious
3. valuable
4. mischievous
5. energetic
6. athletic
7. starry
8. humorous
9. angelic
10. friendly

Exercise 64

1. tempestuous
2. poisonous
3. miraculous
4. sensible (senseless)
5. metallic
6. influential
7. ancestral
8. accidental
9. industrial
10. expensive

Exercise 65

1. miserable
2. cautious
3. courageous
4. favourable
5. skilful
6. disastrous
7. angry
8. grievous
9. picturesque
10. fabulous
11. fortunate
12. natural
13. vigorous
14. circular
15. methodical
16. criminal
17. sympathetic
18. furious
19. customary
20. wintry

Exercise 66

1. Siamese twins
2. Persian lamb
3. Parisian fashions
4. Alpine climbers
5. Venetian canals
6. Israeli oranges
7. Viennese dances
8. Tibetan monks
9. Finnish athletes
10. Icelandic trawlers

Exercise 67

1. French
2. Spanish
3. Danish
4. Swedish
5. Venetian
6. Dutch
7. Italian
8. Norwegian
9. Belgian
10. Canadian

Exercise 68

1. Irish humour
2. Swiss lakes
3. the Egyptian people
4. a Mexican village
5. the Greek king
6. Belgian chocolates
7. Portuguese wine
8. the Scottish Highlands
9. the Maltese population
10. a Manx cat

Exercise 69

1. Hungarian
2. British
3. Turkish
4. Brazilian
5. Sicilian
6. Pakistani
7. European
8. Cypriot
9. Iraqi
10. Ghanaian
11. Neapolitan
12. Japanese
13. Genoese
14. Czech
15. Portuguese

Exercise 70

1. greedily
2. heartily
3. cleverly
4. sweetly
5. thoughtfully
6. easily
7. hungrily
8. hurriedly
9. comfortably
10. fiercely

Exercise 72

1. gracefully
2. heatedly
3. gratefully
4. longingly
5. proudly
6. attentively
7. reverently
8. respectfully
9. thoroughly
10. loyally

Exercise 73

1. fought heroically
2. listened intently
3. paused momentarily
4. waited patiently
5. gave generously
6. spoke fluently
7. promised faithfully
8. fell awkwardly
9. wandered aimlessly
10. arrived punctually

Exercise 74

1. politely
2. carelessly
3. bitterly
4. sadly
5. cautiously
6. suitably
7. strongly
8. frequently
9. abruptly
10. kindly
11. fatally
12. promptly

Exercise 75

1. stealthily
2. frantically
3. angrily
4. correctly
5. comfortably
6. breathlessly
7. immediately
8. rapidly
9. fearlessly
10. skilfully

Exercise 76

1. hurriedly
2. easily
3. peacefully
4. hopefully
5. accidentally
6. sleepily
7. scornfully
8. mentally
9. proudly
10. heroically

Exercise 77

1. The pilot said that he had made a forced landing.
2. The children cried when they were scolded.
3. Dorothy's mother asked her to dust the lounge.
4. The captain told the crew that he wanted to speak to them when the ship docked.
5. The queen said that she had a severe headache.
6. The matron ordered the nurses to report to her when they went off duty.
7. Judith said that she would be meeting a friend of hers.
8. Robin took one look at the gun and saw that it was his.
9. The surgeon told Mrs. Cook that he would operate on her immediately.
10. The police informed the jeweller that they had arrested the man who had robbed him.

Exercise 78

1. his
2. hers
3. yours
4. ours
5. mine
6. theirs

Exercise 79

1. I
2. me
3. me
4. I
5. me
6. me
7. I
8. me
9. me
10. I

Exercise 80

1. and
2. for (as; because)
3. whether
4. until
5. while
6. unless
7. if
8. although
9. because
10. but

Exercise 81

. Handel was a famous composer who wrote some of the world's greatest music.
. At the museum we saw a sword which had belonged to Lord Nelson.
. I have just sold the book which I bought yesterday.
. There is the policeman to whom I gave the watch I found.
. At the police station there was a man whose house had just been burgled.

6. A large crowd watched the steeplejack who was seated on top of the church tower.
7. We saw the jet fighter which crashed in a field behind our house.
8. Next door to us lives a boy whose father is a circus acrobat.
9. Jean resembles her mother, from whom she gets her good looks.
10. The clerk was robbed of a suitcase which contained the wages of the staff.
11. I am sure this is the film that Jane told us about.
12. The police took charge of the little child that had lost its way.

Exercise 82

1. in
2. at
3. across
4. behind
5. through
6. during
7. under
8. from
9. over
10. to

Exercise 84

1. along
2. over
3. between
4. over
5. over
6. among
7. in
8. into
9. up
10. with
11. at
12. past
13. beside
14. besides
15. for
16. on
17. with
18. against
19. from
20. from

Exercise 85

1. to
2. with
3. from
4. with
5. to
6. with
7. of
8. of; to
9. with
10. of
11. with
12. on
13. of
14. on; upon
15. into

Exercise 86

1. Alan; Michael
2. France; British; American
3. Mount Everest
4. Yesterday; I; Mother; I
5. At; William; The Inchcape Rock
6. Suddenly; Barry; Has
7. Every; Easter; Janice; Eastbourne
8. The; Buckingham Palace; Westminster Abbe
9. Christmas; Jesus Christ
10. Up; Down; We; For
11. Grandpa; The Daily Globe
12. I; Robinson Crusoe

Exercise 88

2. Norway
4. Birmingham
5. Alfred
6. Stonehenge
7. Atlantic
8. Spaniard
14. Aladdin
15. Dutch
17. Sussex
19. October

Exercise 89

1. does
2. is
3. comes
4. likes
5. come
6. like
7. was
8. Doesn't
9. put
10. is
11. are
12. has
13. was
14. is
15. shocks
16. was
17. was
18. was
19. are
20. is

Exercise 90

1. doesn't
2. has
3. were
4. Doesn't
5. hasn't
6. do
7. Were
8. was
9. were
10. has
11. take
12. were
13. hasn't
14. weren't
15. Does
16. doesn't
17. were
18. were
19. were
20. go

Exercise 91

1. was
2. has
3. has
4. has
5. has
6. was
7. has
8. has
9. were
10. gets
11. have
12. is
13. takes
14. Has
15. was
16. was
17. was
18. has
19. Does
20. has

Exercise 92

1. No
2. Yes
3. No
4. No
5. Yes
6. No
7. Yes
8. Yes
9. Yes
10. No

Exercise 93

1. St. Paul's Cathedral was built by Sir Christopher Wren.
2. Sheffield is noted for the manufacture of fine cutlery.
3. William Caxton set up the first printing press in this countr
4. The whale is not a fish but a mammal.
5. The kangaroo carries its young in a pouch.
6. Snails are used for food in France.
   (In France snails are used for food.)
7. The elm tree has a very rough trunk.
8. The earthworm will eat all kinds of decaying leaves.
9. Eskimos go fishing in frail skin canoes called kayaks.
10. The eagle seizes its prey with its strong talons.

Exercise 98

1. F
2. D
3. E
4. H
5. I
6. J
7. B
8. A
9. C
10. G

Exercise 99

1. "Has morning come already?"
2. "Your dinner is ready, Ronald,"
3. "What are you doing here?"
4. "I can run faster than any boy in school,"
5. "As soon as Mr. Joyce comes I shall be going out,"
6. "What terribly rough weather we are having this week
7. "Does Mrs. Phillips live here, please?"
8. "Oh, please let me go,"
9. "Susan's apple is bigger than mine,"
10. "Here's Ralph. Let's hide behind this bush,"

Exercise 100

1. "Tending your horse, sir?"
2. "Ship ahoy!"
3. "What do you mean by making the water in the stream muddy?
4. "Stand under the window and hold up your cap."
5. "That's quite enough—I hope I shan't grow any more."
6. "Does the King live here?"
7. "John Ward, who blacked your face?"

8. "You know that you are not allowed to fish from the bank opposite the school, Brown?"
9. "A thousand thanks Mr. Pinocchio for having spared me the trouble of breaking the shell."
0. "Please Mummy, may I have five pence to buy some chocolate?"

Exercise 101

1. "There," said the schoolmaster, as they stepped in together, "this is our shop, Nickleby."
2. "That's the judge," said Alice to herself, "because of his great wig."
3. "My address," said Mr. Micawber, "is Windsor Terrace, City Road."
4. "Hallo!" growled Scrooge, "what do you mean by coming here at this time of day?"
5. "Come along," shouted Peter to Heidi, "we have a long way to go yet."
6. "Ride her!" I cried with the bravest scorn. "There never was a horse upon Exmoor foaled I could not tackle in half an hour."
7. "O, Father," sobbed Maggie, "I ran away because I was so unhappy."
8. "Go and poke the fire, Martin Rattler," said the schoolmaster, "and put on a bit of coal."
9. "Perhaps it has been buried for ten years," whispered Mistress Mary. "Perhaps it is the key to the garden."
0. "Call off thy dogs," warned Little John, "or they are likely to be hurt."

Exercise 102

. Mr. Watkins asked Kenneth if he had posted the letters.
. Uncle James remarked that it was raining cats and dogs.
. The headmaster announced that school would reopen on September 3rd.
. Her mother asked Janet if she would help to make the beds.
. Dr. Anderson told Stephen that the medicine would soon put him right.
. Mrs. Duncan asked Maisie if her mother was at home.

7. Mrs. Higgins complained to the grocer that the eggs were not fresh.
8. Bernard's father warned him not to burn his fingers with the fireworks.
9. Mr. Trent inquired if anyone had seen his daily paper.
10. The drowning man shouted for help.

Exercise 103

1. "Have you read Oliver Twist, Rodney?" asked his teacher.
2. "This cushion is too hard," complained Grandpa.
3. "I feel tired and will go to bed," said Wilson.
4. "The cabins are flooded!" reported the seaman.
5. "I shall be ninety next birthday," remarked Mrs. Hollins.
6. "I have just found a pound note, Roger," said Dennis.
7. "It is ridiculous to expect a child to do three hours' homework!" exclaimed Father.
8. "The Harvest Thanksgiving Service will be held on September 21st," announced the vicar.
9. "Why were you absent yesterday, Ruth?" asked her teacher.
10. "Will you mend the hole in my pullover, Mother?" asked Raymond.

Exercise 104

1. arch; herald; jolly; marble; zebra
2. dainty; inkwell; plague; trough; youth
3. chair; glacier; nerve; rake; wheel

4. march; measles; middle; monk; music
5. defend; ditch; dormouse; drag; duke
6. halt; heart; hinder; horse; hurry

7. drain; dress; drill; drop; drudge
8. flash; flesh; flint; flour; flush
9. space; spend; spill; sponge; spur

10. shrapnel; shred; shrink; shroud; shrug
11. broad; broke; brook; brother; brown
12. lance; land; lane; language; lantern

13. strict; stride; strike; string; stripe
14. straggle; straight; strange; strap; straw
15. portable; porter; portion; portmanteau; portrait

Exercise 105

1. It's	It is	6. we're	we are
2. There's	There is	7. I'm	I am
he's	he is	you're	you are
3. I'll	I will	8. what's	what is
4. Here's	Here is	can't	cannot
I've	I have	9. shouldn't	should not
5. I'd	I would	10. We'll	We will

Exercise 106

1. You are	You're
2. We have	We've
3. You had	You'd
4. would not	wouldn't
5. is not	isn't
6. do not	don't
7. has not	hasn't
8. shall not	shan't
9. must not	mustn't
10. does not	doesn't
11. Who has	Who's
12. There will	There'll
13. Who would	Who'd
14. have not	haven't
15. She will	She'll
16. could not	couldn't
17. were not	weren't
18. will not	won't
19. I am	I'm
20. are not	aren't

Exercise 107

1. its; it's
2. whose
3. haven't
4. it's
5. whose
6. aren't
7. who's
8. doesn't
9. Who's; whose
10. don't

Exercise 108

1. undress
2. unhappy
3. ungrateful
4. unarmed
5. uncertain
6. unhealthy
7. unconscious
8. untrue
9. unpopular
10. unskilled

Exercise 109

1. inexpensive
2. indirect
3. injustice
4. incorrect
5. insane
6. invisible
7. inattentive
8. incomplete
9. inoffensive
10. incurable

Exercise 110

1. dishonest
2. disappear
3. disobedient
4. disagree
5. discourteous
6. disarm
7. disrespectful
8. discontented
9. disconnect
10. disarrange

Exercise 111

1. painful
2. powerful
3. harmless
4. useless
5. thankful
6. careless
7. cheerful
8. helpless
9. doubtful
10. pitiless; powerful
11. restless; sleepless
12. skilful
13. plentiful
14. successful
15. homeless

Exercise 112

1. immovable
2. irregular
3. non-intoxicating
4. nonsense
5. impure
6. illegal
7. impossible
8. improbable
9. non-essential
10. impolite
11. illegible
12. impatient
13. illiterate
14. imperfect
15. irresistible

Exercise 113

1. friend
2. selfish (mean)
3. timid
4. humble
5. cowardly
6. multiply
7. hinder
8. poverty
9. defence; defend
10. hatred
11. victory
12. knowledge
13. reveal
14. failure
15. opaque
16. folly
17. narrow
18. giant
19. straight
20. disperse

Exercise 114

1. seldom (rarely)
2. maximum
3. departure
4. exterior
5. permanent
6. modern
7. blunt
8. retreat
9. worse
10. coarse

Exercise 115

1. expand
2. permit
3. opaque
4. cautious
5. extravagance
6. gradual
7. compulsory
8. captivity
9. modest
10. superior

Exercise 116

1. comic; tragic
2. admit; deny
3. artificial; genuine
4. assemble; disperse
5. barren; fertile
6. create; destroy
7. assistance; hindrance
8. internal; external
9. command; obey
10. majority; minority

Exercise 117

1. alive
2. last
3. wrong
4. question
5. foolish
6. scarce
7. safety
8. shallow
9. spendthrift
10. guilty

Exercise 118

1. dirty
2. timid
3. solid
4. early
5. short
6. found
7. awake
8. empty
9. curse
10. hurry
11. quiet
12. false
13. cheap
14. heavy
15. broad
16. front
17. giant
18. proud
19. peace
20. enemy

Exercise 119

1. plentiful
2. see
3. pitiful
4. sad
5. top
6. sleepy
7. oils
8. empty
9. strong
10. obtain

Exercise 120

1. misfortune
2. brave
3. famous
4. jolly
5. doubtful
6. shortage
7. impudence
8. weariness
9. lazy
10. forbid

Exercise 121

1. start
2. scatter
3. sly
4. seize
5. serious
6. smell
7. surprise
8. show
9. still
10. stop
11. sailor
12. snug
13. scarce
14. sign
15. scare
16. strong
17. still (silent)
18. sorrow
19. sudden
20. select

Exercise 122

1. dawn; sunrise
2. splendid; gorgeous
3. decrease; dwindle
4. foremost; leading
5. fortunate; lucky
6. enmity; hostility
7. edge; brink
8. loiter; linger
9. invincible;
    unconquerable
10. loathe; detest

Exercise 123

1. round
2. leave
3. least
4. began
5. brave
6. waste
7. tried
8. anger
9. drink
10. ghost

Exercise 124

1. cheat
2. short
3. smell
4. anger
5. steal
6. begin
   (start)
7. horse
8. angry
9. brave
10. drunk
11. rough
12. error
13. ghost
14. force
15. speed
16. waste
17. small
18. scorn
19. still
20. young

Exercise 125

1. weak
2. torpedo
3. tall
4. assist
5. rowdy
6. strong
7. mass
8. arrangement
9. resurrection
10. praise

Exercise 126

1. E
2. F
3. G
4. H
5. B
6. I
7. J
8. A
9. C
10. D

Exercise 127

1. immediately (instantly)
2. determined (decided)
3. return
4. librarian
5. useless
6. Suddenly
7. insane
8. correctly
9. dismounted

Exercise 128

1. unwrapped
2. ventilate
3. matron
4. lengthen
5. rescued
6. revolve
7. disappeared (vanished)
8. recently
9. artificial
10. dustman

Exercise 129

1. son
2. dye
3. flue
4. foul
5. hire
6. guilt
7. rein (reign)
8. quay
9. wring
10. knot
11. whole
12. for (fore)
13. reed (red)
14. pause
15. nun
16. would
17. missed
18. plaice
19. tide
20. vein (vane)

Exercise 130

Last week Mother thought she would like to go for a sail on the sea. She heard that two boatmen had just made their boat ready, so she went down to the quay, where she did not have to wait long, for the tide was right in.

Exercise 131

1. plane
2. wring
3. waste
4. muscle
5. piece
6. hour; our
7. currant
8. mane
9. peel
10. route

Exercise 132

1. stake
2. bier
3. gambol
4. serial
5. hoard
6. plaice
7. pray
8. feinted
9. steel
10. hair

Exercise 133

1. boy; buoy
2. course; coarse
3. sail; sale
4. stile; style
5. knew; new
6. bawl; ball
7. crews; cruise
8. board; bored
9. time; thyme
10. their; there

Exercise 134

1. won; one
2. rode; road
3. write; right
4. bear; bare
5. aloud; allowed
6. cheque; check
7. heard; herd
8. maid; made
9. seen; scene
10. grate; great

Exercise 135

1. as cunning as a fox
2. as busy as a bee
3. as brave as a lion
4. as blind as a bat
5. as agile as a monkey
6. as meek as a lamb
7. as playful as a kitten
8. as tender as a chicken
9. as quiet as a mouse
10. as proud as a peacock

Exercise 136

1. as bright as a button
2. as fit as a fiddle
3. as fresh as a daisy
4. as light as a feather
5. as sharp as a razor
6. as round as a barrel
7. as straight as an arrow
8. as sound as a bell
9. as thin as a rake
10. as regular as a clock

Exercise 137

1. two peas
2. grave
3. Job
4. eel
5. rock
6. velvet
7. honey (sugar)
8. ABC
9. vinegar
10. rain

Exercise 138

1. brass
2. berry
3. gall
4. new pin
5. doornail
6. cucumber
7. dust
8. pancake
9. crystal
10. gold
11. large
12. happy
13. hungry
14. stubborn
15. strong
16. keen
17. sharp
18. safe
19. deaf
20. thick

Exercise 139

1. as black as coal (pitch)
   as white as snow
2. as hot as fire
   as cold as ice
3. as rich as Croesus
   as poor as a church mouse
4. as hard as nails (iron)
   as soft as putty
5. as strong as a horse (an ox; Samson)
   as weak as a kitten (water)
6. as slow as a snail (tortoise)
   as quick as lightning
7. as heavy as lead
   as light as a feather
8. as drunk as a lord
   as sober as a judge
9. as thin as a rake
   as thick as thieves
10. as tough as leather
    as tender as a chicken

Exercise 140

1. . . . ends well.
2. . . . than never.
3. . . . no robbery.
4. . . . first served.
5. . . . twice shy.
6. . . . sweep clean.
7. . . . pound foolish.
8. . . . run deep.
9. . . . think alike.
10. . . . less speed.

Exercise 141

1. Look
2. while the sun shines
3. Necessity
4. Empty vessels
5. Absence
6. at home
7. Imitation
8. Pride
9. play
10. another

Exercise 142

1. E
2. I
3. F
4. J
5. H
6. B
7. A
8. D
9. G
10. C

Exercise 143

1. A cat may look at a king.
2. Enough is as good as a feast.
3. Exchange is no robbery.
4. Hunger is the best sauce.
5. Look before you leap.
6. Where there's smoke there's fire.
7. One man's meat is another man's poison.
8. One swallow does not make a summer.
9. Out of sight, out of mind.
10. What's sauce for the goose is sauce for the gander.

Exercise 144

1. to take the bull by the horns
   (to meet difficulties or dangers boldly)
2. to paddle one's own canoe
   (to do things for oneself)
3. to blow one's own trumpet
   (to boast about oneself)
4. to be a dog in the manger
   (to deny to others what is useless to oneself)
5. to sit on the fence
   (to refuse to take sides in a dispute)
6. to strike while the iron is hot
   (to act while conditions are favourable)
7. to put the cart before the horse
   (to do things the wrong way round)
8. to let the cat out of the bag
   (to disclose a secret)

Exercise 145

1. F		6. H	
2. E		7. A	
3. I		8. J	
4. G		9. D	
5. B		10. C	

Exercise 146

1. to keep it dark
2. to pay through the nose
3. to be at loggerheads
4. to give a person the cold shoulder
5. to feather one's nest
6. to make a mountain out of a molehill
7. to swing the lead
8. to throw cold water on it
9. to send to Coventry
10. to have a bone to pick with someone

Exercise 147

1. mouth (to live only for today, with no thought of tomorrow)
2. horse (to do work which produces no results)
3. bee (to be possessed by a crazy idea)
4. water (to get into trouble)
5. music (to take punishment or criticism without complaint)
6. cloud (to be under suspicion)
7. leaf (to lead a new life)
8. breast (to confess to some wrong)
9. ends (to live within one's means)
10. second (to take a back place while someone else leads)

Exercise 148	Exercise 149	
1. baggage	1. kin	11. fame
2. foot	2. call	12. free
3. key	3. tongs	13. facts
4. ruin	4. starts	14. chop
5. nonsense	5. tear	15. sixes
6. span	6. sure	16. rough
7. nail	7. file	17. safe
8. go	8. square	18. fast
9. means	9. sweet	19. hale
10. shoulders	10. blood	20. young

Exercise 150

1. Darby and Joan
2. hammer and tongs
3. hue and cry
4. down and out
5. young and foolish
6. cats and dogs
7. neck and neck
8. hale and hearty
9. spick and span
10. rack and ruin

Exercise 151

1. time and time
2. thick and thin
3. heaven and earth
4. body and soul
5. high and low
6. ups and downs
7. well and good
8. heart and soul
9. long and short
10. give and take

Exercise 152

1. pack
2. peel
3. queen
4. solid
5. exterior
6. niece
7. class
8. cygnet
9. drought
10. hoof

Exercise 153

1. arrow
2. cub
3. princess
4. smell
5. airport
6. import
7. leg
8. insect
9. flowers
10. suit (coat)

Exercise 154

1. sculptor
2. gloves
3. scales
4. rind
5. beaver
6. teacher
7. tea
8. elephant
9. captain
10. ascend

Exercise 155

1. patient
2. fingers
3. poetry
4. did
5. train
6. pork
7. France
8. flowers
9. sky
10. scabbard

Exercise 156

1. payable
2. responsible
3. advisable
4. divisible
5. inseparable
6. indigestible
7. perishable
8. reversible
9. inaudible
10. irritable

Exercise 157

1. burglar	11. councillor
2. bugler	12. reporter
3. cobbler	13. pillar
4. tailor	14. register
5. grammar	15. bachelor
6. radiator	16. corridor
7. cellar	17. regular
8. popular	18. docker
9. decorator	19. doctor
10. beggar	20. scholar

Exercise 158

1. February
2. separate
3. receipt
4. address
5. Wednesday
6. library
7. jewellery
8. surprise
9. secretary
10. accommodation

Exercise 159

1. niece
2. friend
3. field
4. weird
5. Believing
6. thief
7. seized
8. piece
9. yield

Exercise 160

1. hideous
2. commence
3. traitor
4. government
5. jester
6. Saturday
7. cemetery
8. wintry
9. favourite
10. extension

Exercise 161

1. calm
2. wrinkles
3. gnawing
4. knuckles
5. wreck
6. knitted
7. knowledge
8. ironing
9. psalm
10. pneumatic

Exercise 162

A	B
1. rare	1. stoop
2. parrot	2. open
3. trapper	3. stamp
4. Pope	4. notice
5. party	5. motion

C	D
1. miner	1. greed
2. inner	2. erase
3. noon	3. stream
4. trained	4. scourge
5. motor	5. stamen

Exercise 163

1. street
2. sister
3. draper
4. nought
5. rounder
6. tablet
7. centre
8. invent
9. strong

Exercise 164

1. versus
2. postcard
3. Esquire
4. caught; bowled
5. horse power
6. kilometres per hour
7. born; died
8. page
9. care of
10. Her Majesty's Ship

Exercise 165

1. British Broadcasting Corporation
2. Medical Officer of Health
3. General Post Office
4. Cash on delivery
5. United Nations Organisation
6. Greenwich Mean Time
7. Limited; Established
8. Automobile Association
9. National Society for the Prevention of Cruelty to Children
10. Justice of the Peace

Exercise 166

1. and other things
2. by way of
3. per annum (yearly)
4. of this month
5. Postscript
6. Note well
7. Queen Elizabeth
8. namely
9. in the year of Our Lord
10. before noon

Exercise 167

1. Worcestershire v. Kent
2. Nottinghamshire v. Hampshire
3. Essex v. Glamorgan
4. Yorkshire v. Surrey
5. Lancashire v. Gloucestershire
6. Wiltshire v. Cambridgeshire
7. Lincolnshire v. Buckinghamshire
8. Berkshire v. Staffordshire
9. Bedfordshire v. Suffolk
10. Hertfordshire v. Cornwall

Exercise 169
(Possible answers)

1. clean; queen; scene
2. clear; queer; sphere; steer;
3. hurt; shirt; alert; skirt;
4. bore; four; roar; tore; pour; soar
5. goal; hole; bowl; coal; pole; foal; mole;
6. purse; verse; worse; curse;
7. jerk; work; shirk
8. drum; some; thumb; glum; come; crumb
9. roam; home; comb; foam; Rome;
10. goes; rows; nose; toes; bows; rose; foes; mows; hose

208

Exercise 170

1. witches
2. ditches
3. battle
4. cattle
5. plain
6. rain
7. eye
8. by

Exercise 171

1. light
2. night
3. snow
4. blow
5. spray
6. day
7. cheery
8. aweary
9. best
10. rest

Exercise 172

A. I wandered lonely as a cloud
That floats on high o'er vales and hills,
When all at once I saw a crowd,
A host of golden daffodils.

B. Fair is the land of hill and plain,
And lonesome dells in misty mountains;
And crags where eagles in tempest reign,
And swan-loved lakes and fountains.

Exercise 173

1. palace
2. hole (nest)
3. burrow
4. den
5. shell
6. holt
7. stable
8. cell
9. web
10. drey
11. nest
12. form
13. rectory
14. convent (nunnery)
15. den
16. lair
17. vicarage
18. fold (pen)
19. sett
20. parsonage

Exercise 174

1. kennel
2. pigsty
3. lodges
4. holt
5. hutch
6. eyrie
7. form
8. dovecote
9. lair
10. sett

Exercise 175

1. log cabin
2. barracks
3. convent (nunnery)
4. manse
5. monastery
6. Palace
7. prison

Exercise 176

1. kitten
2. piglets
3. lamb
4. cubs
5. calf
6. goslings
7. tadpoles
8. chicks
9. kid
10. duckling
11. filly (colt)
12. elver
13. cygnet
14. eaglets
15. fawn

Exercise 177

1. hissed
2. squeaking
3. trumpeted
4. squealed
5. bleated
6. howling
7. chattering
8. cawing
9. purred
10. hooting

Exercise 178

1. bay
2. twitter
3. cackle (hiss)
4. gobble
5. growl
6. screech
7. crow
8. low
9. chirp
10. coo
11. frogs
12. horses
13. donkeys
14. hens
15. bulls
16. hyenas
17. bees
18. beetles
19. apes
20. lions

Exercise 179

1. tick
2. creaking
3. patter
4. wailed
5. peal (clap)
6. shriek
7. skirl
8. whirr
9. clatter
10. call

Exercise 180

1. clang
2. beat
3. whack (swish)
4. rumble
5. singing
6. popping
7. grinding
8. swish
9. rustle
10. jangle (rattle)
11. coins
12. bullet
13. gun
14. feet
15. bow
16. horn
17. saw
18. rifle (gun)
19. steam
20. whip

Exercise 181

1. postman
2. jockey
3. clown
4. auctioneer
5. chimney-sweep
6. artist
7. photographer
8. conductor
9. policeman
10. miner (collier)
11. blacksmith
12. cobbler

Exercise 182

1. butcher
2. fishmonger
3. fruiterer
4. confectioner
5. clothier
6. tobacconist
7. florist
8. chemist
9. grocer
10. stationer

Exercise 183

1. ironmonger
2. carpenter
3. dentist
4. tailor
5. artist
6. doctor
7. cobbler
8. steeplejack
9. surgeon
10. plumber

Exercise 184

1. sculptor
2. shepherd
3. glazier
4. pilot
5. barber
6. chauffeur
7. milliner
8. caddie
9. undertaker
10. tinker

Exercise 185

1. sailor
2. doctor
3. lawyer
4. dentist
5. policeman
6. chemist
7. detective
8. artist
9. organist
10. clergyman

Exercise 186

1. cashier
2. caretaker
3. newsagent
4. porter
5. reporter
6. architect
7. commercial traveller (salesman)
8. saddler
9. detective
10. greengrocer

Exercise 187

1. traitor
2. drunkard
3. stowaway
4. pilgrim
5. martyr
6. conscript
7. hermit
8. cannibal
9. hypocrite
10. eavesdropper

Exercise 188

1. Austin . . . . . . bankrupt
2. Bell . . . . blackleg
3. Cook . . . . optimist
4. Dawson . . . . miser
5. Evans . . . . . bachelor
6. Farley . . . . . glutton
7. Grey . . . . spendthrift
8. Hawkins . . . . vegetarian
9. Ingram . . . . . patriot
10. Jenkins . . . . . . emigrant

ANSWERS TO
COMPREHENSION EXERCISES

Comprehension 1

PIP SMOKES A PIPE

1. Pip saw a young man seated at the foot of a tree puffing at a pipe.
2. It made Pip want to smoke.
3. The heat of the day made the young man so tired.
4. After yawning the young man put down his pipe on the grass and fell asleep.
5. Pip snatched the pipe from the grass and ran away with it.
6. His mother and brothers laughed because they saw clouds of smoke pouring from his mouth.
7. Pip's father warned him that he would one day turn into a man.
8. Pip took the pipe out of his mouth and did not smoke it again.

Comprehension 2

THE OLD MAN OF THE SEA

1. The old man wanted the writer to carry him over the brook.
2. The writer had pity on him because of his age.
3. He twisted his legs tightly round Sinbad's neck.
4. He dug his feet into Sinbad's stomach to make him rise and carry him further.
5. The old man opened his legs to let Sinbad breathe more easily.
6. Sinbad had left some grape juice in the calabash and it had become wine.
7. The wine gave him fresh strength.
8. After drinking the wine he danced and sang with right good-will.
9. Sinbad killed the old man with a big stone.
10. The sailors told Sinbad that he was the first person they had known to escape from the old man of the sea.

215

Comprehension 3

ALICE AND THE WHITE RABBIT

1. Alice was sitting on the bank.
2. Her sister was with her.
3. Her sister was reading.
4. Alice was not interested because the book had no pictures or conversations in it.
5. She considered making a daisy-chain.
6. She felt very sleepy and stupid because the day was so hot.
7. The White Rabbit's eyes were pink in colour.
8. "Oh dear! Oh dear! I shall be too late."
9. The White Rabbit took a watch out of its waistcoat-pocket.
10. It went down a large rabbit-hole under the hedge.

Comprehension 4

TOM AND THE POACHERS

1. He was unable to sleep because the moon shone so brightly through the water.
2. The beautiful sight Tom saw was a bright red light.
3. Tom swam to the shore to see what it was.
4. He saw five or six great salmon underneath the light.
5. He rose to the surface of the water to look more closely at this wonderful light.
6. When he reached the surface he heard a voice say, "There was a fish rose."
7. Three great two-legged creatures stood on the bank.
8. One of these carried a light, and another a long pole.
9. Tom longed to warn the foolish salmon.
10. Before Tom could make up his mind to do it a salmon was speared right through and lifted out of the water.

THE BREAD-FRUIT TREE

1. broad; long; smooth; glossy; deeply indented (three required)
2. The fruit is like wheaten bread in appearance, and is round in shape.
3. It is very important to the natives because bread-fruit is their principal food.
4. The fruit hangs on the branches in clusters of twos and threes.
5. A ripe bread-fruit is yellow in colour.
6. The bread-fruit tree produces two or three crops of fruit in a year.
7. It was twenty feet above the ground.
8. The bark of the young branches is used by the natives for making cloth.
9. 'Pitching their canoes' means making them watertight. The gum of this tree is used instead of pitch.
0. 'durable'

TAMING A WILD HORSE

1. After going boldly up to the wild horse Dick patted its head and stroked its nose.
2. Nothing is so likely to alarm a horse when someone approaches as any appearance of timidity or hesitation.
3. The horse eyed him nervously all the time.
4. Dick carried the water in his cap.
5. When Dick offered him a drink the horse sniffed suspiciously and backed a little.
6. He buried his lips in the water and sucked it up.
7. Dick went up to his shoulder, patted him, undid the line that fastened him and vaulted lightly on his back.
8. This made the horse plunge and rear a great deal.
9. Dick urged the horse into a gallop over the plains.
0. The horse smelt his new master all over.

Comprehension 7

THE ISLE OF PALMS

1. The pirates proceeded to take in those stores of which they stood in need.
2. They travelled in a schooner.
3. Palm trees grew on the shores of the harbour.
4. The palm trees grew sufficiently high to prevent the ship's masts being seen from the other side of the island.
5. Manton did not wish the captives to see what he was doing.
6. Here lay the wreck of what had once been a noble ship.
7. The pirates constructed a rude tent or hut on the green knoll near the margin of the bay.
8. An old sail and some broken spars were used in constructing it.
9. They left their captives a small cask of biscuit.
10. The jailer warned the captives not to cross the island to the bay in which the schooner lay.

Comprehension 8

LION COUNTRY

1. The party halted soon after sundown.
2. They halted by the side of a wood.
3. The edges of this place were composed of dense thorns.
4. Three sides of the square patch were made up of thorns.
5. The waggon formed the fourth side.
6. It was made to protect the horses and bullocks from wild beasts.
7. The bushes they cut down were used to fortify the lower part of the waggon.
8. The General suggested making this enclosure.
9. The word 'lions' made Dinny appear to be turned into stone.
10. Dinny worked with feverish haste, bullying Coffee and Chicory for not bringing in more dead wood for the fire.

Comprehension 9

MR. CREAKLE

1. The banquet was held in the dormitory.
2. David Copperfield paid for it.
3. Mr. Creakle slashed his pupils unmercifully every day of his life.
4. He had been a small hop-dealer in London before taking up teaching.
5. Mr. Creakle brought Mr. Tungay with him because he had broken his leg in Mr. Creakle's service.
6. Mr. Tungay regarded the masters and pupils of the school as his natural enemies.
7. J. Steerforth was never punished by Mr. Creakle.
8. When the eating and drinking were over most of the guests went to bed.
9. The rest remained whispering and listening.
0. Mr. Tungay's only delight in life was to be sour and malicious.

Comprehension 10

MUSKRAT CASTLE

1. A waggish officer had given the castle its name.
2. It was a quarter of a mile from the nearest shore of the lake.
3. The eastern shore was the nearer.
4. The house was supported by piles driven into the shoal.
5. The water immediately beneath the house was six to eight feet deep.
6. The shoal ran in a north and south direction.
7. It was a few hundred yards long.
8. Hutter had built his house on the shoal in order to be safe.
9. Hutter had no sons when he went to live in Muskrat Castle.
0. He was well supplied with arms and ammunition.

Comprehension 11

SAVED FROM THE CRUEL SEA

1. The loud report of a cannon caused the windows of the cottage to shake.
2. The noise appeared to come from near the cliff.
3. They saw rocket after rocket whizzing high in the air.
4. Paul and Ned saw a revenue cutter on the Iron Rock.
5. The blue light was extinguished by a wave.
6. It was caused by the mast falling over the side of the ship.
7. Six men were clinging to the mast.
8. Paul and Ned took two coils of rope with them.
9. The only survivor was a negro boy of about fourteen.
10. He slept in the kitchen of a nearby cottage.

Comprehension 12

THE BELL ROCK COLLECTION

1. The procession was held to collect money to fix a bell on the dangerous rock.
2. Perth and Dundee
3. The monks chanted in the procession.
4. Seamen carried the flags and banners.
5. The patron saint of sailors is St. Antonio.
6. The coins were collected by little boys.
7. They were dressed as angels.
8. An adventurous young seaman had proposed fixing the bell.
9. They gave generously because there were few who had not to deplore the loss of someone dear to them.
10. The rock was dangerous because it lay in the very track of vessels entering the Firth of Tay.

THE CHILDREN'S OCCUPATIONS

1. The children had to remain in the cottage so that the troopers would not find them.
2. Their father had been killed by the troopers.
3. The children would have been burnt in their beds if Jacob had not taken them away.
4. Their real surname was Beverley.
5. The surname Jacob told them to use was Armitage.
6. Edward was chosen to go hunting with Jacob because he was the oldest.
7. Humphrey had to look after the pony and the pigs.
8. Jacob, Edward and Humphrey
9. Humphrey fetched water from the spring.
10. Edith had to feed the fowls and collect the eggs.

THE DESTRUCTION OF POMPEII

1. They heard the crash of falling roofs.
2. The mountain-cloud seemed to roll towards them.
3. A shower of ashes mixed with fragments of burning stone came out of the mountain-cloud.
4. The shower of ashes and stone fell with a mighty splash into the agitated sea.
5. Safety for themselves was the sole thought of the crowd.
6. Some thought there would be a second earthquake.
7. They hastened to their homes to load themselves with their most costly goods.
8. Others rushed under the roofs of buildings to escape the showers of ashes which fell in torrents on the streets.
9. Pompeii was a coastal town. The ashes fell into the sea.
10. groans; oaths; prayers; shrieks

Comprehension 15

BUILDING AN IGLOO

1. The Eskimo used a knife for drawing the circles.
2. The diameter of the larger circle was seven feet, and of the smaller one four feet.
3. The smaller circle was two feet to one side of the larger one.
4. The blocks of snow were arranged in a circle.
5. Soft snow was used to fill in the chinks between the blocks.
6. The last block of snow fulfilled the purpose of a keystone.
7. The larger igloo was finished first.
8. There were two doors in the larger igloo.
9. The windows were made of slabs of clear ice.
10. The igloos were connected by an arched passage.

Comprehension 16

EXPLORING AFRICA

1. He took up his lodging for the night at a small village.
2. He gave his horse some corn to eat.
3. He was told that he would see the River Niger.
4. Lions were numerous near this place.
5. The gates were shut a little after sunset.
6. The thought of seeing the Niger and the buzzing of mosquitoes prevented the writer from sleeping that night.
7. He was ready before daylight.
8. He had to delay his departure until the gates were opened.
9. They carried the various articles they were going to sell at Sego market.
10. When the writer saw the river he drank some of its water and gave thanks to God.

Comprehension 17

IN A HINDU TEMPLE

1. After making his purchases Passepartout took a ride through the city of Bombay.
2. A Parsee festival was being held there that day.
3. When he got near the pagoda he wanted to see the interior of it.
4. They are expected to leave their shoes at the door.
5. Passepartout was lost in admiration of the gorgeous ornamentation.
6. Three priests attacked him as he was looking round.
7. They tore off his shoes and stockings.
8. After getting to his feet Passepartout knocked down two of his adversaries and rushed out of the pagoda.
9. One priest pursued Passepartout.
10. He managed to escape by mingling with the crowd.

Comprehension 18

THE LEPER

1. The incident took place in the early morning.
2. Gorse grew on either side of the footpath.
3. A white hood covered his head.
4. The covering was not pierced with eye-holes because the leper was blind.
5. He gave warning of his approach by ringing a bell.
6. He felt his way along the path by tapping with a stick.
7. Matcham wanted to run away because he believed that the touch of the leper meant death.
8. He thought it unnecessary because the wind was blowing away from them and because the leper was passing by.
9. As he drew level with the pit the leper paused, and turned his face full upon the lads for some seconds.
10. After crossing the little heath the leper disappeared into the woods.

Comprehension 19

CROSSING THE ANDES

1. Mariano Gonzales had travelled with the writer before.
2. They carried a great deal of food in case they should be snowed up.
3. They cooked their food in an iron pot.
4. They bought firewood, hired pasture for the animals, and bivouacked in the same field with them.
5. 'under a cloudless sky'
6. A madrina is an old steady mare with a bell round her neck.
7. The madrina is useful because the other mules follow her.
8. The old mule will track out the madrina by the power of smell.
9. Four of the mules were needed to carry the food.
10. Six were used for riding.

Comprehension 20

ATTACKED BY ROBBERS

1. John Ridd was returning from Porlock market.
2. Six other farmers were riding with him.
3. The Doones had no grudge against John Ridd because he never flouted them.
4. His companions pulled out their money.
5. John Ridd set his staff above his head and rode at the Doone robber.
6. The name of his horse was Smiler.
7. John saw a dozen robbers.
8. No, some of the robbers were on foot.
9. The rest of the robbers drew their horses away.
10. He was crouching by the peat-stack.